CREATING TEACHABLE MOMENTS

A Guidebook to Inspiring
Values in the Classroom

Dr. Shannon W. McPherson

Creating Teachable Moments

A Guidebook to Inspiring Values in the Classroom

Dr. Shannon W. McPherson

Copyright ©2024 Dr. Shannon W. McPherson

Neuroplasticity Publishing

Tomball, Texas

Cover design by Pankaj Singh Renu

Edited by Ita de Groot

First Printing

The information given in this book should not be treated as a substitute for professional medical advice; always consult a medical practitioner. Any use of information in this book is at the reader's discretion and risk. Neither the author nor the publisher can be held responsible for any loss, claim, or damage arising out of the use or misuse of the suggestions made, the failure to take medical advice, or for any material on third-party websites.

ISBN: 979-8-9897371-3-0

Library of Congress Control Number: 2024910391

shannonwmcpherson@gmail.com

http://www.docmcpherson.com

Dedication

I dedicate this work of passion to the most important people in my life.

Paul, thank you for your support, love, and patience as I spent endless hours researching, discussing, and writing this work of art.

To my children, Krystalynn and Austin, for believing in me as I traverse a new beginning.

To my parents for their love, support, and guidance throughout my life.

To past, current, and future students. I have written this book so that I may find a way to enhance your spirits as you move through the challenges that life will always bring about.

Table of Contents

Introduction

Phones out, heads down, glazed looks. Sound familiar? Unfortunately, this scene is all too familiar in most classrooms, and it's a problem.

I've been a high school classroom teacher for twenty-six years and have witnessed an inverse relationship between student attitudes and my age. Attitudes toward hard work, authority figures, and appropriate behaviors have taken a steep downturn as my experience has increased. As a result, each day has become more difficult in the classroom. It feels like there's a constant battle with the use of phones, homework completion, lack of attention during class, inadequate respect, and decreased resiliency to setbacks.

As a teacher, have you ever experienced being out of the classroom due to illness? Did you return to a messy classroom with only a handful of students completing the assignments left for them? Have you asked the students why? Did you get answers like "I didn't know" or "I didn't feel like doing it"? This had grown into a routine in my room, and I became exasperated.

1

Despite grading consequences and personalized discussion, it continued to occur regularly whenever I had to be out of the classroom for any reason.

This reminds me of the wilted and dry herbs I once saw outside a local grocery store. They were uncared for and unnurtured and they demonstrated this with drooping leaves, portraying sadness. I'm a plant person, and this really bothers me, so when I say dying plants remind me of my classroom, you know I mean business.

I have ruminated over these glaringly obvious issues, which were increasingly becoming problematic, much like the dropping of leaves from one of the beloved plants I keep on my desk at school. Don't get me wrong. I rarely have had severe behavioral issues in my classroom, but something was missing, and I couldn't put my finger on it. It felt like a word on the tip of my tongue that wouldn't erupt from my vocal cords. A lack of determination, a lack of community, a lack of trust, tolerance, and respect. Basically, a lack of compassion for self and others. I'm not just talking about students, but educators, too.

What had happened to the trusting, reflective, respectful classroom of yesterday? The classroom where both teacher and student wanted to be? What happened to the students who wanted to learn and reach toward the sky in search of a better life? What happened to teachers who had the courage to allow their students to think openly and freely?

During the course of my career, I have become increasingly concerned due to students appearing unmotivated, seemingly without purpose or drive. One of my junior students refused to put her phone away despite a strict rule regarding phones in class. She was always glued to the screen and would become irate if I asked her to put it away. She didn't complete classroom assignments and rarely completed her homework. This progressed to parent discussions and administrative actions. During a meeting with her parents, she stated that she felt as if her future aspirations were worthless in today's world. In effect, she felt jaded.

It felt as if the search for true meaning and purpose in life had been erased, just as my student claimed.

Each day felt as if new possibilities were stripped away, and teaching from the heart was considered overrated. It seemed as if the search for true meaning and purpose in life had been erased, just as she claimed.

Has the quest for greatness disappeared from our current society? Is this why some people have been leaning toward superficial "quick" fixes? Fast and immediate "feel good" moments? If this is happening in the world around us, how do I, as a responsible and resourceful teacher, mitigate this injustice toward my students in the classroom?

In my search for an answer, I spent a great deal of time speaking with fellow educators, meditating on the subject, visiting a plethora of websites, and rereading several how-to-teach books I keep on my bookshelves at home. Many of these books guide teachers on how to do activities and expose students to content aligned with the curriculum. These are important tools to support student learning, such as where to place an ivy plant for growth, but they didn't answer my questions. Something had been missing in the average classroom over the last few years. Something emotional, even psychological.

As I continued researching, I learned that over 800,000 people died by suicide in 2016 across the globe, and according to the Centers for Disease Control website, in 2019, more than 36 percent of high school students felt sad or hopeless. Over 18 percent seriously considered suicide. This is a very serious public health issue, and teachers are stuck in the middle of this ongoing battle for the souls of their schools and students. Just how do we rejuvenate the sickly plants in our care?

In response to my concern, I began to include my students on a personal mindfulness journey so they could feel better about themselves and work on their well-being. According to *The Inner Curriculum*, "Wellbeing can be defined in two ways: firstly, a background state of mind that each of us generally feels about our life; secondly, a more transient, fluctuating state of mind that depends on the availability of a range of psychological, social, and physical resources we need to meet life's challenges" (Hawkes, 2018). At the time, I thought students needed to work on calming their minds with a few minutes of mindfulness activities each day to increase their well-being, like adding a bit of water to my pothos ivy plant. In my first book, *My Teachable Moments*, I discuss mindfulness and how I implemented meditation, yoga, observation of feelings, gratitude, and the celebration of friendship. You can find this book on my website, www.docmcpherson.com.

It seemed to tame some of my concerns about student behavior and their feelings of worthiness by bringing a bit of calmness to their demeanor, but it wasn't "cutting it." I began to skip mindful moments a few days a week due to my lack of motivation and lack of student attention while performing the activities. The gratitude writing exercises had become empty pieces of paper, and students wouldn't celebrate friendship with others. This was bothersome, and I became determined to analyze more data, read more books, and find new tactics to help my students become better learners, better community members, and simply feel better about themselves.

I was growing increasingly frustrated and began looking forward to each weekend and holiday as I marked an "X" through each day on my classroom calendar. It felt like a countdown to escape.

One day, while I was intentionally not thinking about student and teacher concerns, I was busy washing dishes in my kitchen at home while listening to an audiobook. It came to me. One word erupted from my subconscious. It was as if a streak of sunshine exploded out of dark, ominous clouds.

A word. Just one word. *Values.*

I dropped a glass in the sink in awe, soap and water splashing on the counter. I dried my hands and began to brainstorm the topic with pen and paper. This brought about many questions. Philosophically, what are values? How would I bring this to my classroom without causing turmoil with parents due to misunderstandings? How do I, as a teacher, responsibly integrate this ever-increasingly important topic into my daily curriculum?

After brainstorming thoughts and questions, I went online, googled "values education," and came upon Dr. Hawkes' work on values-based education. I promptly ordered several books and consumed everything I could find on the website. That same day, I also discovered Parker J. Palmer's *The Courage to Teach* books, ordered them, and spent considerable amounts of time on that website, too. It was like I had found an intensive plant care book with lifesaving tools that could work to stimulate a plant to thrive again.

As part of my research, I discovered the true meaning of values and came up with a battle plan to involve the vocabulary as described in *From My Heart* by Dr. Hawkes (2013). Fear began to bubble in my gut as I realized that I may have issues with the curriculum being covered in a timely manner and that I may have pushback from colleagues, administration, and peers.

I imagined arguments with peers over this issue and discussions about how I should only teach science, not values, with administrators. This grew into a personal quandary and true fear of student indifference and their potential lack of response to my efforts. As this fear grew, I realized I was fearful of failing, just as I had felt had occurred with the mindfulness journey. I decided to stop my endless endeavor of hope, and I put the books away and closed the values-based education website tabs that were always open on my personal computer. I continued with the usual educational dogma that had been ingrained into my brain, and I chose not to nourish my poor pothos ivy plant.

A few weeks later, a late arrival showed up in my mailbox. A back-ordered book was finally received. A glimmer of hope was sparked in my heart as I began to read *On the Subject of Values…and the Value of Subjects*. On page 32, a statement caused a shiver up and down my spine. It read, "Values enable children to learn more deeply. They infuse and guide the learning dimensions that make up the whole picture of a successful learner. These learning dimensions enable a learner to make sense of subject disciplines, make meaningful connections between areas of learning, and to better understand themselves and their world" (Knight, 2022).

My fears lifted, and I was once again determined to bring values into the classroom.

After deep reflection and self-analysis of my own value system, I decided to integrate terms in the classroom verbiage that reflected my values. I purposely and openly modeled those same values in coordination with the mindfulness journey I began with the students at the beginning of the school year. I became excited as I began to use value words during class as part of the content being covered.

As the year carried on, students began telling me how they used breathing techniques to make it through a difficult situation in another classroom, how they started practicing yoga at home to help wake up in the morning, and how the use of self-reflection solved conflicts with peers. By integrating values lessons as part of the mindfulness journey, students were reaping the rewards, and I saw my pothos ivy begin to grow, vining across my desk and lab station, bringing greenery and beauty to my classroom.

As I tried to spread my newfound teaching technique to colleagues, my earlier fears were brought to life. My teaching partners were not "hip" with the idea, which led to excuses such as "I don't have time" and "I don't believe that will help behavior." I remitted and continued on my own within forty-five-minute class periods, six times a day, five days a week.

After reading about values-based education and continuing to research through innumerable Google searches, I knew that it would take a village to make sustainable changes that would benefit both the student and the teacher. I needed a village of like-minded educators in today's society who were willing to look within themselves to define their own values, then look into the community and determine a standard of values that each child could express and integrate into their life—values that would give our children the tools to be courageous as they strive to achieve personal responsibility. Values that would help our students become honest, kind, compassionate, respectful, and resilient. Essentially, a perfect environment for the metaphorical pothos ivy plant on my desk.

The goal of this book is to encourage educators, parents, students, and communities so that values can be assessed and implemented as part of the curriculum—not set apart from daily classwork. It is an inspirational dialogue for those who wish to provide more than an objective-based curriculum in the classroom, a road map of how to use accepted societal values in the classroom as a learning tool. Essentially, it is the plant book I referred to earlier—a guide for growing big, beautiful pothos ivy plants.

It is a book that will help you establish the classroom you have dreamed of—one that is full of respect, the love of learning, and impactful connections made honestly and compassionately. This is a handbook that is healthy, both physically and emotionally, for both you as the educator and the learner as the student.

Each chapter will cover value-terminology verbiage that is essential throughout most communities. That value will be discussed philosophically to provide context and explanation. Reflection exercises have been provided in each chapter that will add a deeper level of understanding for you as the teacher. These exercises can help you model the values discussed in and out of the classroom as you develop your personalized techniques as part of the learning process. They can also be adapted for use with students. You will watch your pothos ivy grow and prosper as you learn and implement the lessons discussed throughout this book.

"The ultimate measure of a man is not where he stands in moments of comfort and convenience but where he stands at times of challenge and controversy. The true neighbor will risk his position, his prestige, and even his life for the welfare of others. In dangerous valleys and hazardous pathways, he will lift some bruised and beaten brother to a higher and more noble life."

Martin Luther King, Jr.

Chapter 1

Transformation

Are you frustrated with today's youth in the classroom? I know I have been in the past, and I blamed the students for being lazy, the administration of my school for being inadequate, the parents for a lack of involvement, and society for allowing children to behave without remorse. There seemed to be no recourse for me as a teacher to counter the woes I felt. Even with years of experience, I personally felt at odds with what I saw in the classroom, stories I heard from colleagues, and news stories of youth breaking laws and wreaking havoc. My pothos ivy was leggy, dropping leaves, and appeared to be dying, as was my passion for the classroom.

My School Year from Hell

It is mid-March. I sit at my desk, answering an email, and the bell rings. Students are still meandering in the hallway, slowly sauntering to class. An announcement is heard over the intercom: "Students, it's important that you get to class on time.

Teachers, please step into the hallway and help direct students to their classrooms." I look up, walk to the door, look at the large number of students slowly walking down the hallway, and close my door.

I start class by telling the students to turn in their homework. Two of the twenty-five students on my roster walked to the front of the class to turn in the assignment. I sigh and put the papers away in a folder to be graded later.

Once again, I start class only to be interrupted multiple times by students entering late. One girl sneaks in, thinking she is unnoticed, and four more students sign in as tardy. I repeat that homework is due, and for a third time, try to start class only to be interrupted by another announcement about checking the students for ID badges and proper dress. I roll my eyes, look at the calendar, and mentally count the days until Friday.

I begin to discuss the subject I had planned to teach and realize that most of the students have their phones and are distracted by whatever is on their screens. I had tried to start with a strong no-cell phone policy that year and was frustrated by what I saw. I remind them to put their phones away, and while waiting for them to do so, I take attendance. Five students are absent, and five are tardy. Of the twenty-five students on my roster, one student has not been to class in over a week.

I turn in my attendance, walk to the front of the room, and realize that several students have chosen to keep their phones in their laps. They intentionally try to hide their phones from me, and I remind them to put up their phones as requested and reinforce that phones must be put away in order for me to start class. They complain but follow my instructions.

12

It is now fifteen minutes into a forty-five-minute class period. I only have thirty minutes left to cover the topic for the day and pass out an assignment. This assignment would become homework due to a lack of time—a homework assignment that would probably not be completed.

I am finally able to start the lesson at this point. I lecture and struggle to get the students interested by asking questions. Most are quiet, withdrawn, and refuse to raise their hands or answer questions. The two students who are active in the class answer without raising their hands and take over the discussion. I am grateful for their participation, but the rest of the class mentally checks out from the learning I am trying to impart.

I then hand out the assignment, give verbal instructions, and return to my desk. I look at the calendar again and count the days until the next big break as the students look into their laps at their phones.

This is not the classroom I visualized as a young teacher early in my career. I had visualized respect for rules, authentic excitement, student contribution, and a collaborative atmosphere. I had expected students to share with peers as part of their learning and apply themselves as they used creativity to solve problems with enthusiasm. I had foreseen that my love for learning would flow into the souls of the students in each of my classes.

I didn't expect the lack of respect, withdrawal from reflection, and lack of care I had now witnessed and experienced. I had reached a low point in my career as a teacher, and I felt that I didn't have the tools to control the chaos in my microcosm of a world, and it was frustrating.

As the school's year-end approached, I adoringly looked past my sad pothos ivy at the calendar multiple times a day as summer advanced. I was frustrated and exhausted. I was not certain if I would return the following school year.

For the next few months of school, these actions I told you about earlier were repeated six times per day. It was a struggle, and I felt my heart was breaking. Since I was nearing retirement age, I began looking forward to the time when I wouldn't have to deal with students as I admired my retired colleagues on social media. They had escaped the drudgery of a teacher's life, and I was quite jealous.

At last, summer arrived, and I was free!

As the days of summer swam by quickly, I spent time reading and reflecting on the past school year. I had a few weeks to decide if I would continue teaching the following year, and I was determined to see if I could find a solution. I wanted to see if there was something I could do within the microclimate of my classroom that would help students trust me, reflect upon their learning, and show respect and compassion for each other.

I ran across this quote, and it resonated in my soul: "The children now love luxury; they have bad manners, contempt for authority; they show disrespect for elders and love chatter in place of exercise. Children are now tyrants, not the servants of their households. They no longer rise when elders enter the room. They contradict their parents, chatter before company, gobble up dainties at the table, cross their legs, and tyrannize their teachers." My head nodded in agreement. I then read who was given credit for this statement. Plato credited it to Socrates, who lived 469–399 BC.

A Revelation

This was a big aha moment for me. It wasn't our current lifestyle and community that we all live within that was causing issues with the students; it was me, and something that I lacked was affecting my students. My complaints were the same as those of the great teachers of yesteryear, and I was resolute in my endeavor to find a way to give students something to look forward to as they entered my class. I was looking for a way to revitalize my little pothos ivy plant. They needed a reason to want to be in my classroom, to want to learn, to want to reflect on that learning, and to want to be a part of something bigger than themselves.

As I read and delved into the issue, I sought out tools to help me cope, such as journaling, self-reflection, and meditation. I was embarking on a mindfulness journey as I fought to keep my passion for teaching alive. Teaching was part of me, part of my being, and part of my soul, and I didn't want to give it up. Just the thought of not returning to school the following year would bring about depressive thoughts despite my frustration with the previous school year.

I became more and more determined to find tips, tricks, and techniques to experiment with to have a cohesive class structure that had meaningful moments each day. I wanted to create a place that I had visualized many years previously. During those summer months, I felt I had replenished my toolbox and anticipated a school year full of positivity and joy.

Once the new school year commenced and the honeymoon of the first two weeks was over, my pothos ivy was thriving but then started to wilt as I noticed the students slipping back into behaviors observed from the years before. I was resolved to not let this occur, and I began sharing my mindfulness journey as well as utilizing the tips, tricks, and techniques I had discovered over the summer. I had a bit of success, and it felt good. Students who had begun to be tardy each day started to arrive on time. Questions in class became discussions, and homework was being turned in on time. It was much better than the previous year, but I still felt something was missing.

After discovering values lessons and overcoming my associated fear, as discussed in the Introduction, I began to implement lessons to instill those values. I had always modeled my expectations in the classroom, but I discovered that I should model my core values for the students. I was open and honest with them about my classroom experiment and expressed my own struggles with humility. In the past, it was considered a weakness to show students vulnerabilities, and I had adhered to this belief, so becoming more human in front of my students was a challenge. As a role model in a values-inspired classroom, students should know it is natural to work through self-improvement. The reasoning is simple: if you don't work on it, you can't improve. I felt similarly to Parker J. Palmer's statement in *The Courage to Teach*: "By finding a place in the ecosystem of my reality, we might see more clearly which actions are life-giving and which are not—and in the process participate more fully in our own destinies, and the destiny of the world, than we do in our drive for control" (2017). I didn't want control. I wanted to make a difference in a healthy way as a partner with my students. I wanted to revitalize their interest in education and give them the nutrients to grow to their full potential. I wanted them to feel the love for learning that I felt.

I began to witness a newfound vitality in the classroom. Students were thinking of their own value system and began putting phones away, paying attention during lectures, and asking relevant questions throughout the lessons. They felt more connected as they worked in collaborative groups and established a sense of belonging. Students demonstrated trust by asking me to watch their second backpacks and hold onto their lunches during the day, and they expressed their ability to pause and self-reflect during challenging moments at school. They showed tolerance and inclusion with their peers and felt true acceptance to be themselves courageously and creatively. My students were becoming more resilient to setbacks as they began to embrace responsibility in a patient way. They began to truly trust me, trust each other, and trust themselves.

A sense of calmness descended upon the atmosphere of the classroom, and I was lucky enough to have an administrator observe the change in demeanor and attitude as students entered my classroom. I witnessed compassion that I had not seen before, and my classroom was once again a place where people wanted to be and where students wanted to learn. There was an authenticity I had never experienced. My sweet pothos ivy had grown beautifully in a large pot, with healthy soil, adequate light, plenty of water, and room to grow with proper nutrients. It could even be propagated to spread its beauty.

My room became a healthy classroom full of love and learning. It was amazing!

Exercises throughout This Book

As part of learning about integrating values lessons into your classroom, you will spend some time in introspection. This is an important part of learning about values education. As Audrey Hepburn said, "As you grow older, you will discover you have two hands, one for helping yourself, the other for helping others." In order to heal our classrooms and instill much-needed values into the curriculum, we must know what we think and why we think it. Many of the exercises will first help you acquire self-awareness as the teacher and can be modified for use with students.

Journaling Exercise Questions:

These questions apply to you as a person but can also be modified for use in the classroom with students.

1. Do you remember a rough school year? Think about that time frame for a few minutes.

   a. How did you cope during that time?

   b. How did it make you feel?

   c. Brainstorm the factors that played a role in the unpleasantness that enfolded that school year. Write down everything that comes to mind.

2. Remember a pleasant or good situation that you have encountered at school. You can even remember a positive school year.

   a. How did that make you feel at the time?

   b. Brainstorm the factors that played a role during that school year. Write down everything that comes to mind.

3. Answer the following questions:

   a. Why are you reading this book? What are you wanting to gain?

b. Do you have specific goals you would like to achieve as you read this book? Have you thought about how you wish to achieve these goals?

After answering the questions above, take a short break to reflect on what you have written. If you are working individually, add any additional notes that may come to mind. If performing this exercise in a group or with students, have another member of the study group share their answers as you listen without judgment, and then you do the same.

Value Exercise Conclusion

How do you feel about this exercise? Did it cause you discomfort as you reminisced about the negative situation asked in question number one? Did you smile when you thought about the pleasant situation? Seemingly simple, but not so simple, self-reflection questions can cause discomfort, and some of the questions used in this book are meant to be uncomfortable in the quest for self-awareness and growth.

Chapter 1 Summary

I discussed the trials and tribulations I underwent during a funky school year and briefly covered how I turned that negative experience into a positive one using values lessons, modeling, and implementation of these values.

Many teachers have not been able to create the classroom they visualized early in their careers. There are many challenges to this endeavor, and this book will help you build an atmosphere of comradery, trust, and compassion. The remaining chapters in this book will discuss specific values such as trust, reflection, compassion, respect, collaboration, tolerance, resilience, and connectedness. Each chapter's title is the core value being discussed, and I integrate additional values into each chapter. For example, tolerance, inclusion, and acceptance are all related and discussed in Chapter 8. These priceless values will be weaved together, and we will watch our pothos ivy plant grow to its greatest potential of green gorgeousness.

Join me as we get started by defining and discussing values. What are they, and how do we determine our personal and professional values? And why is this important?

"The greatest discovery of all time is that a person can change his future by merely changing his attitude."

Oprah Winfrey

Chapter 2

Values

Dream with me.

Envision a perfect classroom.

Desks or tables are neatly arranged in rows, clean counters shine, and your desk is organized. The room is freshly dusted, swept, and mopped, smelling of cleanliness and the excitement of a new day. It is a welcoming environment. A pleasing environment that is conscientiously arranged for ease of movement and comfort of students. There are pictures and positive affirmations on the walls and images that depict your preferences. Your pothos ivy is lush and green, spreading its lovely vines of leaves down the front of your desk.

Lesson plans and expectations for the students have been designed with student access in mind. You are at ease as you look around your classroom and smile, fully expecting a wonderful day to unfold.

The bell rings.

Students respectfully enter the classroom with smiles of anticipation on their faces. They are openly curious to learn about the day's activities, and it shows in their positive demeanor. You welcome them at the door with smiling eyes, perhaps a handshake, and an honestly felt "Good morning." The students also greet you with enthusiasm and optimism as they ask you about your day.

They move to their seats, read the objectives and agenda on the front board, and prepare for class by putting cell phones away and gathering supplies such as notebooks, paper, computers, and pens. The bell rings, students are in their seats, and all eyes are on you as you take attendance and begin the lesson.

When advised, students begin collaborating with peers as they use creative, critical thinking skills to solve problems and devise solutions in a meaningful way. In core classes, students could be interpreting the text in an English class, performing a science laboratory experiment in a science class, analyzing a historical moment in a social studies class, or solving mathematical equations in a math class. In electives, they could be creating pieces of artwork, pinning material for a sewing project, or even listening to the heart using a stethoscope.

Students of all shapes, sizes, socioeconomic statuses, backgrounds, and learning abilities are working together in self-directed, cohesive groups. They ask you questions as you move through the classroom, modeling leadership and a love of learning. You are a trusted advisor, mentor, and guide as they traverse new material and learn from you and each other.

A phone's alarm goes off, notifying you that the bell will ring in two minutes, letting you and the students know it is time to conclude class activities. They begin straightening the room and cleaning up their areas. Assignments are neatly put away or turned in as expected, and as the bell rings, students respectfully move to their next class as they express gratitude with thank-yous and goodbyes.

Is this a magical realm of wonderment? No, this is a mindful, healthy, respectful learning environment with proactive students who are trusting, compassionate, tolerant, and resilient. This is a place where subjective behaviors and student-centered objectives are met. This is a values-centered classroom. This is my version of heaven in my chosen profession, teaching, and I dreamed of it often while I diligently worked to bring it to fruition during more than twenty years of practice.

What Is a Value?

Before we can go any further, we need to define the word *value*. Values are fundamental beliefs that guide us. They are the personal qualities that motivate our attitudes and actions as we move through life. Our personal value system indicates to the world what sort of person we are. It displays how we treat ourselves and the manner of the way we treat others. According to Tony Robbins' website, "How one's personal values are defined is based on the feelings and sentiments one holds about themselves and the world around them. Personal values can be positive and lead to self-esteem and fulfillment" (2021).

Within the definition of values, there are different types of values, such as personal and societal, and these tend to intertwine. Values help us determine our intrinsic worth in society, and these may be based on religion, laws, and belief systems developed over time. We end up embracing these values and making them our own, but do they serve us? Are they beneficial to us as individuals in the community? Do they serve your students?

Knowing the values to be integrated into the curriculum is metaphorical to the size of the pot for my pothos ivy plant. A small container will suffice, but it indicates a small plant with less greenery and leggy vines. The larger and deeper the pot, the larger and fuller the plant will become. The size of the pot is the foundation for its growth, just as knowing the values we want to ascribe to daily. This may seem like an easy task, but it takes time, reflection, and determination to learn what values we should demonstrate to the world. This requires defining, categorizing, and clarifying our personal values and creating a game plan for integrating them into the classroom.

How Do We Know If Our Values Are Serving Us?

I am aware that values are subjective. My values as a wife, mother, and teacher are probably very different from those of a single male assistant principal on my campus, but there are some core values I'm sure we all can agree upon. Trust, compassion, reflection, respect, tolerance, and resilience are all examples.

How do we know if the values we are living by are honestly useful to us? This is where we spend time and energy to determine if the values we impute daily serve our highest good. This is also where work is required to reference these values and practice acting on them. As educators, how do we know if students are aware of their own personal values? After twenty-six years in education, I've been privy to very few students who know how their values affect them and how to integrate that knowledge into their lives. Most do not have this knowledge, and unfortunately, this also applies to adults.

For example, my personal values involve collaboration, kindness, compassion, and resilience to setbacks. In my memoir, *My Teachable Moments*, I discussed an issue with differing values at a school where I used to teach. Positive collaboration as a team was nonexistent, and I was surrounded by colleagues who didn't value kindness and compassion as I did. This led to strained relationships, negative emotions, and a lack of fulfillment at that school. Despite my love for the students and the relationships I had built with them, I could not continue in such a demonizing atmosphere. I chose to leave and go to another school that had a similar value system as myself and was able to realign with my personal goals and grow as an educator using creativity and teamwork as tools.

The first step is to consider Dr. Hawkes' explanation of what he calls *The Inner Curriculum*. "The Inner Curriculum teaches us how to be conscious about and in harmonious control of our internal world of thoughts, feelings, and emotions, enabling us to respond appropriately and altruistically to others without hurting them or damaging our own sense of self. Indeed, it supports the development of a strong and secure sense of self, which develops the disposition of self-leadership, which sustains wellbeing."

This leads us to the concept of personal well-being. Personal thoughts and feelings of health, happiness, and contentment in all facets of your life are referred to as your well-being. It represents a comprehensive understanding of an individual's quality of life and includes aspects such as physical, mental, emotional, social, environmental, and occupational. It is important to reflect on your well-being so that you can help your students learn to reflect on their state of well-being. Dr. Hawkes goes on to explore the importance of reflection on well-being in *The Inner Curriculum*: "Reflecting on your own well-being you will see why it is so important to help children to develop the ability to be resilient in the face of life's inevitable challenges."

Just how do you do this? How do you determine the foundation for growth and the pot size you want for the pothos ivy plant? Evaluating your core values and level of self-awareness are avenues to determining your true level of well-being. It is important to know yourself and how you react to instances of positivity and negativity. During my mindfulness journey, I discovered that I did not react well to setbacks. Depending on the level of the setback, I would become angry and then allow depression to set in. Over time, with a great deal of patience from my husband, I would finally get to a point where I could haul myself out of the depths of despair. Through self-examination and reflection, I learned what triggers this emotional roller coaster and learned to step back and assess setbacks in a much healthier, self-compassionate way.

There are many benefits to self-awareness. Self-awareness can lead to increased happiness because you will feel fortuitous when you express who you are, and there will be less inner conflict when your external actions are in accordance with your inner feelings. In addition, decision-making is easier because when you know yourself, you will have guidelines to follow to help you solve life's problems. As you get to know yourself, your ability to be compassionate increases, and your stamina levels will increase, making you more resilient.

As Socrates so eloquently stated, "To know thyself is the beginning of all wisdom."

Values and Health

When an individual knows his or her core values and lives by them, it has been shown in a wide variety of studies to help mental and physical health in a positive way. Knowing and writing about important values has been shown to decrease stress, which leads to better brain health. It also bolsters the ability to solve problems, inspires willpower, increases the ability to communicate more compassionately, and enhances relationships with other people.

According to the National Institutes of Health (NIH), there is emerging evidence that indicates that when core values are prosocial—the act of helping other people—physical health can be bettered (Ibanez et al., 2023). A decrease in inflammatory responses and cortisol can lead to improved cardiovascular health, increased oxytocin and progesterone can lead to longevity, and the immune system can improve its function in the human body.

Why Is It Important to Have Self-Knowledge and Define Your Values as a Teacher?

To be an effective values-instilling educator, you must know yourself to model the values you are teaching. Just what are your values, and how do you apply them daily? If respect is a value you wish to embed in your classroom, how are students going to react if you don't show them respect by belittling or yelling at them? This leads to students who will question your teachings. Regardless of the pot size, the pothos will not grow to its full potential.

For example, as I mentioned briefly earlier, I have a very firm no-cell phone policy use during class. In the past, this policy has been modified based on student needs. One of my juniors had a family member who had been taken to the hospital due to health issues. This student was distressed due to her family's insistence that she stay at school until more information had been gathered by the medical team. When she showed up for my class, I let her go to the bathroom to wash her face, and I allowed her to keep her phone on her desk. Her anxiety decreased, but she was still understandably worried. I demonstrated compassion simply by allowing her a moment of respite by going to the bathroom and allowing her to keep her phone during the class period. She knew that I would consider her circumstances due to my daily modeling of empathy and compassion. Unfortunately, she was not afforded this advantage in another classroom, which increased her anxiety exponentially prior to attending my class.

If I had not taken the time to reflect on my values and understand that my values may be different from those of my colleagues, I might have verbalized that I was upset with that disrespectful teacher. This could have caused a rift between the two of us, which wouldn't have been acceptable in a professional environment.

On a personal level, I feel as if I have a deeper knowledge of myself due to spending time in reflection and meditation to determine what is most important to me, and this has been beneficial in all aspects of my life. I am more balanced and feel more fulfilled because I can line up my actions with my values, set goals, and make decisions that align with my core values.

Let's spend time looking at your values as a valuable human in today's world.

Values Exercise:

You will continue journaling with the exercise below as you spend time evaluating your personal values.

1.   Write down your values.

Make a list of all the values that speak to you from the list below. Choose the values that best capture your emotions or actions. Feel free to add any words that apply to you.

Abundance	Confidence
Academics	Connection
Acceptance	Contentment
Accountability	Courage
Achievement	Creativity
Adventure	Curiosity
Ambition	Dependability
Authenticity	Diversity
Belonging	Empathy
Career	Encouragement
Caregiving	Enthusiasm
Caring	Ethics
Charity	Excellence
Collaboration	Family
Compassion	Fairness

Flexibility	Learning
Freedom	Leisure
Friendship	Love
Fun	Loyalty
Generosity	Making a difference
Gratitude	Motivation
Growth	Nature
Happiness	Optimism
Harmony	Open-mindedness
Health	Order
Honesty	Passion
Humor	Patience
Inclusivity	Perfection
Individuality	Performance
Innovation	Personal development
Intelligence	Popularity
Integrity	Power
Intuition	Professionalism
Joy	Punctuality
Justice	Reciprocity
Kindness	Recognition
Knowledge	Relationships
Leadership	Reliability

Resilience	Spirituality
Resourcefulness	Stability
Respect	Success
Responsibility	Thankfulness
Risk-taking	Tolerance
Safety	Traditionalism
Security	Travel
Self-control	Trust
Self-Respect	Understanding
Selflessness	Wealth
Service	Well-being
Sharing	Wisdom
Simplicity	

2. Observe yourself.

For two to three days, pay attention to your decisions at work and home. Write down your major choices and consciously label the values based on the list above. Were you expressing the values that initially resonated with you at the start of this exercise? If not, which ones were you adhering to? Were you happy with the choices you made?

3. Consider role models.

Write down the names of at least five people you admire, respect, or love. Write down the qualities they have that you find commendable. Would you want to mirror those qualities?

4. Think about your life experiences.

Choose one of the best and most fulfilling experiences in your life, as well as one of the most painful experiences in your life. Write a few sentences about those times in your life and list the values that were being expressed.

5. Imagine your perfect future.

Visualize your ideal existence and your desired future self. Make a list of what you would like to experience in your ideal life. Write down the values that are central to this vision.

6. Categorize your values.

Group the values into categories as part of this exercise. For example, you may have chosen professionalism, punctuality, and reliability. These are all related and can be placed in the same category. Or you may have chosen fun, humor, and optimism. These could also be placed in the same category.

7. Determine the main idea of your values.

Select a term that best embodies the collection of words found in each category. To provide more context for the principal value, leave the other words in the group indented below the primary value.

8. Select your top core values.

Sort the most important values by priority. While there is no set number of fundamental values, it's best to keep the list between five and eight. If you have more than eight, consider the values that are most important to you and put this task on hold for a day or two, then revisit it later to determine whether the top core values accurately represent who you are.

After completing the assignment, take a short break to reflect on what you have written. If you are working individually, add any additional notes that may have come to mind. If performing this exercise in a group, have another member of the study group share their answers as you listen without judgment, and then you do the same.

Value Exercise Conclusion

How do you feel about this exercise? Did you fully engage with this self-reflection exercise and consider various aspects of your life, such as your time at work, time spent with family, and your life within your community? Did you gain clarity on your level of self-awareness, well-being, and values? How do you see using this exercise with your students? Could it be a team-building collaboration exercise as you get to know your students within the first few weeks of school? I have used a similar exercise in the past with students, and it was a wonderful experience for both the students and myself.

When I first completed this exercise, I was surprised, but then again not surprised. For example, I was surprised to discover how important creativity and courage are to me, both in my personal life and in my work life. It helped me put my thoughts into words, and it has helped me make better decisions that are aligned with my personal beliefs and behaviors. Keep in mind that values can change with time, and it is a good idea to reflect and reevaluate periodically. I have done this and am happy to say that they have not changed, but as I age, I can see them varying based on fluctuating priorities such as retirement and my new found love of writing.

Chapter 2 Summary

Values are actions that show the people in our communities and our lives what we find most valuable. They simply show what kind of individuals we are to other people. Different people have different values, but as a society, there are common values we should uphold, such as compassion and respect. Assessing our self-awareness of these values occurs as part of self-reflection and leads to a positive feeling of well-being and happiness. Once we have pondered our core values, we can determine how to teach and model them with our students.

Now that we have discussed the purpose of values and decided on the size of the pot for our pothos ivy, our foundation has been put in place. We will now discuss common values that most communities will agree with and how we can use those values in the classroom to benefit students and teachers alike, the first being trust.

> "Your beliefs become your thoughts,
> Your thoughts become your words,
> Your words become your actions,
> Your actions become your habits,
> Your habits become your values,
> Your values become your destiny."
>
> — Gandhi

Chapter 3

Truth & Trust

"First Comes Truth... Then Comes Trust." I don't know where I read that, but it has stuck in my head since first seeing it. Truth and Trust. What are these values, and why are they important? Not just as a teacher in the classroom, but as a person?

George Orwell once stated, "In a time of deceit, telling the truth is a revolutionary act." Between news, social media influences, and false advertising, we rarely know if someone is being honest, so we tend to default to distrust. Distrust is a result of fear. Fear of being betrayed, fear of being victimized, fear of being vulnerable, fear of the unknown. Fear can also occur when we experience something new or different, which can have negative consequences in the present and the future. When we are fearful, we tend to disconnect from the external world and mentally distance ourselves from family, friends, and those who could help, such as teachers and mentors. That fear can keep a person from seeking something new, such as interviewing for a better job, and even keep them from having needed medical tests.

Truth is the soil for our pothos ivy. It is a vital part of the plant's life because the soil holds the plant up to the light and houses the root system. In association with symbiotic bacteria and fungi, these roots transport water and nutrients up through the plant to the tips of its leaves. Soil also supplies a place for the growth of the roots so our plant can grow ever larger as we continue to learn the importance of values education in the classroom.

Since trust involves genuineness in character and having confidence in others, we must show our students that we can be trusted by being truthful and honest in word and deed. We must show them that we are trustworthy to dispel the essence of distrust, an essence that may have built up over a lifetime.

What Is the Nature of Truth?

In order to flourish as humans, we need truth. If we aren't honest in our daily lives, this could lead to disciplinary measures socially, legally, and psychologically. Even though truth is of utmost importance, what is true to one may not be true to another or not true at all. Think of an optical illusion. Two identical objects appear to be different sizes or shapes, but in reality, they're not. Which aspect of the optical illusion is legitimately real? Isn't this up to the viewer and their ability or inability to see properly?

The topic of truth has a long history and is included as a part of epistemology, the philosophical study of human knowledge. Historical documents regarding the argument of truth begin with Epimenides, Plato, Socrates, and Aristotle. It is still a hotly debated topic in philosophy, and since there are a multitude of theories and perspectives on the nature of truth, I'll reduce the huge amount of material to make it more manageable to understand.

These theories involve the "aim of belief"—truth—which is consistently contrasted with falsity, something not aligned with facts. Truth can be absolute or universal, as seen in math equations and scientific laws, such as the law of gravity. Truth can refer to descriptors of reality aligned with facts, such as all matter being made up of atoms. Truth can be relative due to ethical and cultural beliefs as well as family expectations. Truth can also be considered subjective or malleable based on life and personal experience.

Since we are human beings living within communities, I believe that truth pluralism is the most accurate in our lives. Truth pluralism proposes that there are "multiple ways for truth-bearers to be true." Based on our students' background knowledge, culture, and life experiences, their truths may be different from our own. For instance, I taught two siblings for several years. The youngest, a girl, was regularly told to be extremely quiet and respectful of her older brother's study time. When she studied, he was not required to be quiet and respectful of that time, and she was commonly required to babysit her younger brother while studying. Her reality dictated, in her mind, that her studies were not as important as her brother's. This was her truth, and her grades reflected it. She and I had an in-depth conversation about this situation, and she absolutely believed that her studies were not as important as her older brother's. This was her truth, not the truth I believed.

Trust Is Built from Small Moments of Truth

Truth, our pothos ivy's source of nutrients, can be considered as per this statement from BahaiTeachings.org: "The deep resonance we feel in our hearts when we encounter something pure, beautiful, and authentic" (Langness, 2014). How is truth authentic when it is malleable? The reality of truth is that it may be different from one person to another; thus, truth may be interpreted differently by multiple people. So, how do we handle the truth if it is adaptable in the classroom? This is where trust enters the picture because trust requires truth to sustain, continue, and endure.

This reminds me of the sweet story of a girl and her father. A little girl and her father were crossing a bridge. The father was kind of scared, so he asked his little daughter, "Sweetheart, please hold my hand so that you don't fall into the river."

The little girl said, "No, Dad, you hold my hand."

"What's the difference?" asked the puzzled father.

"There's a big difference," replied the little girl. "If I hold your hand and something happens to me, chances are that I may let your hand go. But if you hold my hand, I know for sure that no matter what happens, you will never let my hand go."

Trust has multiple definitions, but they all lead to the same conclusion. Trust is the confidence put in someone or something because of the belief that they can be relied upon. It is a key element of all relationships, both personal and professional, and leads to a feeling of safety and security.

In my twenty-six-year teaching career, students have usually felt that they could trust me. I would admit when I didn't know an answer, and we would research possibilities together. I would have regular policies and procedures and apply them each day. I would upload their grades in a timely manner, and I would answer their questions with my mind and my heart. They trusted that I would provide lessons that would test their intellect, and I would always be gentle with my comments and critique of the knowledge learned in my class.

This trust led to a safe place for my students to learn—a safe place they wanted to be each day. Nearly every school year, I have had a student who would skip other classes or fail the majority of classes but would always attend my class and earn good grades. They simply wanted to be in my room. They trusted me.

Trust requires reliability and honesty in thought and behavior. Trust is making transparent decisions with input from the students. It requires personal integrity, the knowledge of knowing why and how to adhere to moral and ethical principles, such as treating each student equally. Trust requires competence, the knowledge to be able to provide content that is accurate, precise, and inclusive. Trust requires empathy and compassion, the ability to look within and recognize that a student's truth about themselves may be different from what you see and think.

The Science of Truth & Trust

Don't you feel better when you know you can trust someone? How about when you are trusted? In recent years, neuroscience has performed a multitude of studies regarding trust and how it affects our bodies on a physiological level. Surprising results have been found that can explain why we tend to be more creative, plan better, and make more appropriate choices when we trust someone.

Imagine you are with a trusted colleague, you are working on lesson plans together, and both of you are attempting to solve a scheduling problem. A molecule nicknamed the *trust hormone*, oxytocin, increases in your bloodstream. In turn, this causes you to behave in a trustworthy fashion with your colleague. Due to a lack of fear, the amygdala, the part of the brain that is active when you are fearful, is not as active. This causes your colleague to also have higher levels of oxytocin and become increasingly trustworthy as well.

As a result of the flowing abundance of oxytocin, you become more creative and better problem solvers. Less energy is used to activate the amygdala and you physiologically have more brain power in the frontal lobe and other areas of the brain responsible for high-level thinking.

How Are Trust and Truth Intertwined?

I love this statement made in *The Courage to Teach* by Parker J. Palmer: "A good teacher is one who can listen to those voices even before they are spoken – so that someday they can speak with truth and confidence" (2017).

How does this apply? Truth begs to be spoken, and trust allows it. If a teacher listens by opening his or her heart and that teacher allows a student to speak their truth, this, in turn, creates increased trust between the teacher and student.

Truth and trust evolve in a continuous cycle. Truth brings about trust, trust empowers truth, and both require the other to thrive. Being honest establishes credibility and reliability. Trust enables truth because when there is trust, there is authenticity due to people feeling safe with those they trust. This mutually reinforcing cycle of truth-trust-truth forges connections between educators and learners, peers, and community members.

Truth Exercise

Using positive and affirmative verbiage, follow the instructions and answer the questions reflectively in your journal. These questions apply to you as a person, but they can also be used in the classroom with students.

1. Take a deep breath and relax for a minute. After you have relaxed, reflect on how you feel at this very moment and write it down in your journal. Give that feeling an identifying name.

2. When was the last time you had nothing to say? Did it feel awkward? Did you embrace the silence? Jot down a few sentences describing how it felt.

3. Imagine that you are writing to someone you care about. Write down how you really feel. Embrace the truth and honesty of what you write down.

4. What is something that you like about yourself? Show your gratitude for that something in your journal.

5. What is something that you really want? Be honest and truthful as you write it down.

6. How do you know something is false? Consider social media, the internet, friends, and family. Write a line or two in your journal.

After answering the questions above, take a short break to reflect on what you have written. If you are working individually, add any additional notes that may have come to mind. If performing this exercise in a group, have another member of the study group share their answers as you listen without judgment, and then you do the same.

Becoming Trustworthy

According to nwea.org, teachers and students enter into an "implicit social contract" to form relationships with each other. This contract between student and teacher leads to trustworthiness and greater cooperation between students and teachers. Do you feel your students trust you? Have you asked them? I've asked the students for the truth and asked for ways to improve. I've done this anonymously on paper and online with Google Forms. I've asked their opinions, their thoughts, and what I should continue or not continue doing in the classroom. After mulling over their answers, I have been transparent with the students when making different choices in the classroom based on their responses. I openly acknowledged their answers and let them know that I had considered their thoughts and made adjustments. In essence, I have adjusted the soil in the pothos ivy's pot so that it is more conducive to growth.

To become a trusted educator, you must go deeper than making simple connections with students to learn their truths. It requires an optimistic perspective and an attempt to change negative mindsets into positive ones. As a teacher who models the value of trust, you must also trust your students. This is a reciprocal relationship and is dependent on the teacher's personality and how he or she interacts with students daily, but there are general guidelines that one should follow.

1. **Meeting and starting the process of getting to know your students and letting them get to know you.** This is different from "making connections" or the simplistic "get to know your students." It takes time to learn the ins and outs of each student that crosses the threshold of your classroom. If you have a large number of students, this

requires a great deal of work—work that is worth the time. In years past, I've had nearly two hundred students, and it was a challenge to learn their names, much less get to know them all. Here are some techniques that are helpful to start the truth-trust-truth process.

a. Greet the students at the door for the first few weeks of school. Be sure to make eye contact and ask them how they are doing when they enter the room. Really mean it when you ask.

b. Observe students' behavior and body language. Notice attitudes, moods, dress, and demeanor. When you observe something positive, be sure to say something. Everyone likes to be noticed when they have done something good. I've had students stop being tardy to class because of positive affirmations I have thrown their way when they made it to class on time. This is equally important if you notice an issue that may need to be addressed, such as a student being distressed.

c. Questionnaires can be useful. A simple "getting to know you" list of questions is helpful if you have the time to review all of them. I've also had students create note cards with information about themselves, and I used these cards to randomize questioning. For a few years, I created a beginning-of-year project with note cards. We used shaving cream and food coloring to create tie-dyed cards, and I had them laminated. I would then use these cards to randomly call on students in class. It really personalized the "getting to know you" experience, and I could review the card quickly when calling on students.

    d. Make sure your procedures and routines are explained and obvious. This lets your students know that you are organized and that you know how to coordinate the learning environment.

2. Listen to the students. Really listen, even if it is only one or two students per class. This shows you care and are a kind, sincere person.

    a. Spread your interest in listening to students throughout the classroom. It is hard to do this when one or two students dominate the class, but you need to put the dominating students on hold and show compassion and kindness as you listen to the quiet ones. These are the students who don't stand out because they do their work on time and are respectful during class. When this is witnessed by the other students, they learn that you truly care about everyone's well-being, not just a chosen few.

    b. Show that you are authentic in your sincerity by incorporating the student's background knowledge and interests into the conversation. Ask where the cheerleader is going to be cheering that night. Ask the student who is always doodling if they have artwork that they can show you. Ask your theater kid about their role in an upcoming play. Ask your reader what he or she is reading.

    c. Discover your student's passions. Find your artists, your poets, your thespians, your athletes, your gamers, and your readers. Once you start looking, you will find them. This is a form of listening, and when you honestly see the students, you can create lessons that play on their interests.

3. Show your passion and commitment.

    a. Have fun while teaching. Express your excitement and let your students know why you enjoy your job.

    b. Walk around while you are lecturing and point out how great an answer is when a student is working on an assignment. Always give feedback, either verbal or nonverbal.

    c. Laugh at yourself and laugh with the students. As discussed in my first book, *My Teachable Moments*, humor can be healing.

    d. Be available for the students. Be on time and prepared for class. If you have a tutorial schedule, always be where you say you are going to be. If a student is reaching out for help, be a reliable resource.

    e. Develop creative lesson plans with meaningful assignments; this shows commitment to their learning.

4. Be fair and honest with your students. Nothing dictates distrust more than favoritism, or at least the illusion of favoritism.

    a. Keep your grading policy equitable. If extra credit is offered, it should be available to everyone.

    b. Keep your promises. If you promise to have something graded or completed by a certain date, be sure to keep that promise. Don't agree to something that you know you can't do. If you can't keep that promise, be honest with your students. This shows you are vulnerable as a human with needs. This is another way to develop trust.

c. If you don't know the answer to a question, let them know the truth. Make it a point to learn with your students. I've had students look up answers for me and share them with the class. It's funny how fast they type on their laptops when the teacher doesn't know an answer!

5. Show gratitude and appreciation. Everyone loves to be appreciated.

a. Make it a point to let your students know how much you care about them. This isn't meant to be a lovey-dovey type of statement. It is meant to show gratitude. Students teach us as much as we teach them.

b. Showing appreciation can be a big statement in front of the class; it can also be nondescript. It can be applause for a student stepping outside of their comfort zone, an exclamation of joy when a student tries something new, or it can be a knowing glance with a nod acknowledging a student for their efforts.

c. Don't forget about the quiet ones! They also need to be shown appreciation for their place in the classroom. Too often, our boisterous students steal our attention, and the quiet wallflowers fade away. We don't see their need for sunshine from a trusted teacher.

Trust Exercise

Asking about trusting yourself is an important inquiry that can lead to self-reflection and deeper self-awareness. Answer the following questions reflectively in your journal. These questions apply to you as a person but can also be used in the classroom with students.

1. Have you ever struggled with trusting yourself? Jot down a time when you didn't trust yourself at some point in your life. How did you overcome it?

2. Have you struggled with self-doubt and second-guess your decisions? Write a line or two about this and how you resolved the issue.

3. Write about a time when intuition led you to an answer. Were you surprised?

4. Have you ever closed your eyes and became quiet as you reflected on a situation that required trusting yourself?

After answering the questions above, take a short break to reflect on what you have written. If you are working individually, add any additional notes that may have come to mind. If performing this exercise in a group, have another member of the study group share their answers as you listen without judgment, and then you do the same.

Truth and Trust Exercises Conclusion

Have you learned something you didn't know about yourself? Did the exercises make you feel as if you were expressing your truth, or did the questions make you feel uncomfortable? If they made you feel uncomfortable, how so? These were designed to be used as self-reflective so you could gather more self-awareness to assess your well-being.

Chapter 3 Summary

Trust is difficult to attain without a semblance of truth. Truth has a variety of definitions, but the one that applies best is that truth is malleable and based on a person's life experiences. Trust is built from truth, and we must increase our self-awareness by reflecting on what truth and trust mean to us as individuals. By listening, showing our passion, being fair, and expressing gratitude, students learn to trust us, and we become trustworthy adults. Our pothos ivy is thriving in the knowledge of our core values and has ample, healthy trust to help it grow.

Now, we will move on to another common value that needs to be addressed within ourselves and within our students: reflection. What is it, and how can we use it to increase the well-being of ourselves and our students?

"The dream begins with a teacher who believes in you, who tugs and pushes and leads you to the next plateau, sometimes poking you with a sharp stick called 'truth'."

Dan Rather

Chapter 4

Reflection & Meditation

My alarm goes off four minutes before the bell, earlier than usual, so we can reflect on what was covered in class. I announce that we will quickly reflect on the day's lesson, and I pull out a laminated note card covered in artwork and quickly review the student's personal information. "What is something you now know you didn't know before we started covering this topic?" The student I call on looks at me and tells me a fact that was learned. I have her pull another card from the stack, and I ask that student, "What do you feel about the topic we have been covering?" I then have that student randomly pull another card, and I ask, "What is something you would like to know about this topic that you don't know right now?" Students are engaged, listening, and pondering the questions internally. We are reflecting as a class, and it is a powerful tool that I have always loved using with my students. It helps students achieve a deeper understanding of the material and brings to the forefront a growth mindset as the students share their feelings, what they learned, and what they still wish to learn.

The reflection I am referring to in this chapter is somewhat different from the reflection recollected above. The ivy has spread its vines due to a pot of core values and healthy soil of truth. Now, we are applying the light needed for our metaphorical, nicely growing pothos ivy. But before I get to the self-reflection and awareness I plan to address in this chapter, let's discuss how reflection is typically used in the classroom as a tool or technique to enhance learning.

In the texts used to educate teachers, metacognition is described as the process of becoming aware of and thinking about your thinking and your thought processes. According to this description, reflection is a form of metacognition—a valuable tool for a teacher to check in with students daily. It is a way for students to describe their learning, what they learned, and what they want to learn in the future about the topic. It helps students think about their learning and how they can benefit from learning more.

Many teachers in a variety of subjects use it to deepen learning by applying prior knowledge and new skills learned. It can be used as an opener, a lesson enhancer, or as a review regarding a topic to learn what was known, what is now known, and how that knowledge can be used. Some use it as a writing exercise or as a think-pair-share activity. I prefer it as a verbal exercise with my students so they can think about their thinking, and I can assess their understanding.

Self-Reflection

Our lives are full of noise. Quite a bit of that noise is in our heads, a result of what the Buddhists refer to as the "monkey mind." On a side note, the coined term monkey mind originates from a story about a pet monkey who wouldn't stop pestering his master, not an evolutionary reference. Random and not-so-random thoughts seep into every aspect of life and rarely allow the sound of silence. Many of these thoughts are fleeting, busy, and perhaps irrational, and we don't take the time to think about those thoughts. Thinking about those thoughts can have profound positive effects on a person since we are constantly bombarded with noise. As a society, we are excessively busy with our world of constant stimulation due to social media, news, TV, and the hustle and bustle of our everyday lives. What can we do to taper these distractive thoughts that tend to increase anxiety and negative feelings?

Self-reflection is the process of looking inside while thinking about an external issue that is influencing us, which can be positive or negative. The process of self-reflection helps to identify weaknesses and strengths that are found within us that we can use to strengthen our expression of our core values. To sincerely reflect is to examine within, without passing judgment, and evaluate one's thoughts and feelings. Students need to learn how to reflect on their thoughts and feelings, how those thoughts and feelings lead to actions, and how those actions affect other people. This is a precious value needed in the classroom to enable our students to become more resilient on their own. In Dr. Hawkes' *The Inner Curriculum*, self-reflection should be the fourth "R" in education, reading, writing, arithmetic, and reflection. According to the aforementioned book, self-reflection "is the means through which we access our internal world of thoughts, emotions, sensations, and feelings and regulate them, which helps us sustain mental health and increases the capacity for self-determination." Why does he believe that self-reflection is vital? Analysis of behavior helps you as the teacher and your students grow as they learn to be active and productive citizens in society. It assists the students in their quest for greater self-awareness and gives them a greater sense of well-being as they realize profound insights that can affect their lives. Among the many positive attributes learned, students learn to take the time to realize what triggers certain behaviors, both good and bad. Unwanted behaviors can be consciously curbed in the most unexpected ways through recognition and action.

For example, a girl in one of my classes was known for starting fights with another girl in the cafeteria. She told me that she would intentionally disrespect this girl so she could fight with her, but one day, she decided to pause and reflect on her behavior toward this other student. As a part of this self-reflection, she realized why she wanted to start fights with the other girl, and she stopped the aggressive behavior. She even apologized to the other student!

In the case of our pothos ivy, self-reflection is the light required—a very special light. A pothos ivy is an understory plant. It cannot tolerate sunlight, but it needs indirect sunlight for ample growth. This filtered sunlight is much like the self-reflection we're discussing because it is specialized for the self to induce growth and the spreading of self-awareness.

Self-Reflection and Meditation

Self-reflection and meditation are similar but different. Self-reflection requires that we engage the mind, and meditation requires that we slow the mind to reap the benefits. When we reflect, we are deliberately setting aside some time to think about our past actions, current priorities, and future goals. We gain an understanding of our own thinking through self-reflection practice. It gives us insight into our strengths and shortcomings and enables us to comprehend how we function.

Meditation is mostly a passive activity. If we quiet the mind, the rest happens on its own. By practicing meditation, we can improve our focus and composure and gain a deeper comprehension of the nature of reality. Through this exercise, students are given breathing techniques to help them refocus their attention on learning. Meditation fosters a respectful and compassionate community while assisting students in their lives outside of class. It is amazing what a quiet mind can foster!

Self-reflection with meditation can also allow deep insight into our thoughts, words, and deeds. As the practice of reflective meditation becomes more comprehensive, we become increasingly adept at identifying our thoughts, feelings, values, and beliefs without passing judgment. We can see these things for what they firmly are. How is this beneficial in the classroom? It helps to facilitate student self-regulation, assists students by refocusing their minds, and even fosters compassion toward others.

Similarities between self-reflection and meditation include the enhancement of personal growth in a variety of ways. These actions can easily be used interchangeably in the classroom since they all include focusing inward to cultivate self-awareness, quieting the mind by stilling chatter, being impartial and nonjudgmentally aware, being present in the moment, and giving insight into a person's thoughts and needs. When a group of students takes the time to breathe and visualize, it is very powerful, both for the student and the community at large, since a deeper connection to self leads to a deeper connection to others.

There are a multitude of websites dedicated to the positive attributes of meditation that provide guided meditation practice. I highly suggest binaural beats of varying frequencies mixed with calming music or sounds of nature, such as ocean waves.

The Science of Meditation

Meditation has many years of scientific research behind its positive benefits. According to the National Institutes of Health, the effects of meditation include stress reduction, decreased anxiety, decreased depression, reduction in pain, improved memory, increased efficiency, reduced blood pressure, reduced heart rate, an increase of gray matter in the brain, and a variety of increases and decreases in hormone levels.

Functional magnetic resonance imaging (fMRI) studies have indicated that areas of the brain that are responsible for attention, executive functioning, self-awareness, self-regulation, and memory formation activated when in a meditative state (Boccia, 2015). Through regular practice of meditation, the brain can rewire itself, strengthen the ability for memory, learning, and self-awareness, and decrease the activities of the sympathetic nervous system. The sympathetic nervous system is responsible for stress responses that help us survive in dire situations. Due to our stress-filled lifestyles, sympathetic overactivation has been linked to long-term disease states such as hypertension, anxiety, a variety of endocrine disorders, and depression. Meditation, when practiced regularly, can benefit your emotional well-being and improve the health of your body.

Pausing as a Daily Practice

I'm standing at the door of my classroom, greeting students as they enter. One of my girls walks toward my class, her eyes red and puffy. She is clearly upset about something. I step aside and give her room to enter the class without blocking her entrance. I walk to her desk and ask what I can do to help her. She puts her head down and ignores my question. The bell rings, and all the other students are at their desks, ready for class to start. The upset student still has her head on her desk, not in an emotional state conducive to learning. I give the rest of the students their assignments and ask them to begin working without my assistance. After years of dealing with angsty teenagers, this is not abnormal, so I walk to her desk, put my hand on her shoulder, and ask her to step outside with me. She stomps toward the door, giving me a nasty look.

As we stand in the hallway, I ask her to breathe in and out a few times, then to pause and reflect for a moment. This gives her a moment to notice what is happening internally and externally. I then give her a pass to go to the restroom to wash her face and continue her self-reflection. Upon her return, she evidently feels better and begins her assignment.

I modeled a healthy way to reflect upon a potentially explosive situation. She followed my lead and learned to be more resilient. An intentional pause with controlled breathing can have significant calming effects on the mind and body. She had learned in my class that pausing before self-reflection can be helpful during stressful events; she just needed a gentle nudge to remember this fact. At the end of class, she had fully recovered and apologized to me for her behavior. She admitted that she had overreacted to a situation with her best friend and simply needed to apologize to her. I told her that her admittance was admirable and that I was proud of the responsibility she had taken as she paused to reflect and rethink her emotions and her actions.

Pausing is taking a moment to stop and listen to your inner thoughts. It is a purposeful action that allows someone to stop, dwell on their thoughts, and calm their mind. Pausing with self-reflection as a secondary action is a potent combination that can lead to a parasympathetic response of the nervous system instead of the sympathetic system continuing to be activated in the body. The parasympathetic response calms the body and is commonly known for "resting and digesting," whereas the sympathetic system of "fight, flight, freeze" is activated during times of stress.

How is pausing like self-reflection and meditation? It is a form of quieting the outer noise and going within for a few minutes to appreciate an inner silence.

Reflective Meditation and Pausing Practice:

Before beginning, read through all the instructions so you can follow them without reading them at the same time. Afterward, you will take a few minutes to answer questions as a journaling exercise.

1. Place your feet on the floor and your hands on your thighs. Just be comfortable wherever you are. Make sure your legs and arms are uncrossed.

2. Close your eyes or soften your gaze as you look down your nose at something in front of you.

3. Slowly take a few breaths. Rectangular breathing can be useful. Imagine breathing in the shape of a rectangle. As you

breathe in, count to four. When you reach the top of your breath, hold it as you count to two. Breathe out as you count to four and hold as you count to two. Repeat this a few times.

4. Bring awareness to your feet and your hands. See if you can feel your heart beating.

5. Sit for a minute and be aware of your thoughts and feelings.

6. Now, push those thoughts and feelings away for just a moment and concentrate on your breathing for another minute.

7. Open your eyes, wiggle your toes, and wiggle your fingers.

8. Grab your journal and answer the questions that follow:

   a. How did it make you feel?

   b. Was it comfortable or uncomfortable? Why do you think it made you feel that way?

   c. Did you feel as if you quieted your mind, or did intrusive thoughts invade? If you were not able to still your mind, that is normal. It takes patience and practice to achieve mental stillness.

After answering the questions above, take a short break to reflect on what you have written. If you are working individually, add any additional notes that may have come to mind. If performing this exercise in a group, have another member of the study group share their answers as you listen without judgment, and then you do the same.

How Have I Used This Value Practice in My Classroom?

I find the actions of pausing and reflective meditation vitally important in my classroom. The students enter frantic from maneuvering through the hallways, and sometimes they'll be apprehensive about their daily lives. Using the pausing technique I referred to earlier can take the edge off a single student's situation, and sometimes the nervous energy of students requires reflective meditation before we can start class. Below is a list of ways I've used self-reflection and meditation in the classroom:

1. Reflective meditation is practiced each Monday in class with my students as part of our mindfulness journey's Meditation Monday. Sometimes, I'll guide their breathing. Sometimes, I'll have them breathe naturally. Other times, I'll have them visualize a beautiful and safe place instead of considering their thoughts and feelings. It all depends on how the students are feeling when they enter the classroom. It only takes a few minutes, and it can change the student's agitated and distraught energy into calmness. This increases their ability to concentrate on the lessons. For more information on Meditation Monday, you can find out how to purchase *My Teachable Moments* by visiting www.docmcpherson.com.

2. During particularly frustrating labs or activities, I'll have the students stop for one minute, close their eyes, and breathe for a minute, then have them carry on with the activity. This quick pause in their thinking will generally alleviate frustration with an assignment.

3. Self-reflection snowballs are fun. I hand a piece of paper to a student with a feeling I have that day, and it's tossed about the classroom. As students catch the snowball of paper, they open it up, read it, and add another feeling to the paper.

4. One-minute paper. Set a timer, and the students write down everything they are feeling. After one minute, I have them reflect on what they have written. I tell them that if it's bad,

they're to tear it up into a bunch of pieces and throw it away, and if it's good, to keep it close to their heart as a reminder for when they need it later in the day.

5. Silent breathing with physical movement breaks. If I feel the students are frustrated or overly stressed during class, I'll have them stand up and walk around the room silently while controlling their breath.

6. Water bottle with glitter. I keep a few bottles of water in my room that have glitter sprinkled in them. Students know that they can grab the water bottle, shake it up like a snow globe, and concentrate on the sparkles as they land at the bottom. This is generally enough of a brain break and gives them time to pause and reflect on their thoughts and feelings for those few minutes.

Self-reflection and Meditation Conclusion

How do you feel about using reflective meditation in class? How can you see yourself experimenting with this mindful activity on a personal basis? What about your students? I can assure you that the use of intentional pausing and moments of reflective meditation will help you balance your teaching abilities, making you even more effective as an educator who focuses on values.

Chapter 4 Summary

Self-reflection is multi-faceted. As a typical activity that occurs in the classroom, it can help students think about what they have learned and what they want to learn as a result of what has been covered in class. Self-reflection is a deeper form of reflection that can be used to realize insights into our behaviors that may have detrimental aftereffects. Self-reflection can be used to control your thoughts about what is going on in your life, whereas meditation is a passive quieting of the mind with a great number of physical and mental health benefits. Pausing in association with self-reflection can help students slow and stop their reactions to conflicts or help them recognize a positive aspect of their reactions to others. Self-reflective meditation and pausing can be very powerful tools to instill values in the classroom.

Our pothos ivy has started to sprout new bright green leaves, and it appears to be healthy. The pot represents our core values, the soil represents trust, and now, reflection is the light that has been applied to our plant. If we keep applying life-giving values to our lovely pothos ivy, it will begin to grow into its potential gloriousness.

We will now move on to compassion. Compassion is a skill that gets better with practice as it is a learned skill. We all need to learn how to be more compassionate in a society that seems to have devalued this trait. Let's see how students can enhance their understanding and use compassion to enhance their lives and those in their lives.

"Knowing yourself is the beginning of all wisdom."

Aristotle

Chapter 5

Compassionate Empathy

The seating in my classroom included stools around large tables. The tables had wheels, but the stools did not. The stools were conducive to collaboration, movement, and lab activities but not made for comfort. They were especially uncomfortable for those who had sustained injuries or had pain in their bodies. During one school year, I had several students with severe knee injuries. One of them stayed in constant contact with me during his absence, so I knew when he would be returning to class. On the day of his return on crutches, he looked in the room, looked at me, and gave me a big, toothy grin. I had brought in a teacher-style soft-sided rolling chair and a step stool for him to use during my class. You see, I had knee surgery the year before and knew of the discomfort he would be experiencing upon his return to school. As he recuperated from his injury and subsequent surgeries, he always made an "ahh" sound as he sat in that chair.

After this student was fully healed, I kept that chair in my classroom. Students shared it with those in pain, whether it be a headache, a sprained ankle, or sore muscles from an extensive workout. I would overhear conversations between the students and watch them roll the chair to the person who needed it the most.

This is compassion at its deepest level. This is recognizing someone's discomfort; this is attempting to feel that discomfort, and this is making an effort to eliminate that discomfort.

This is the water required for our pothos ivy to grow. Along with values, the pot forms the foundation; trust, the soil with its symbiotic bacteria; reflection, the light; our plant needs compassion and water for growth. Without water, the soil becomes dried and compacted, and nutrients can't flow to the leaves. As a result, our pothos ivy will struggle to survive and wilt, wither, and potentially die without life-sustaining water.

What Is Compassion?

The word compassion originates from the Latin roots of *passio*, which means to suffer, and *com*, meaning together. Combining these word roots means to suffer together. Compassion is commonly confused with empathy, which is the ability to share an emotional experience. For example, empathy is demonstrated when you become sad, when a friend is sad, or if someone is angry, you become angry. Compassion is empathy plus a desire to lend a hand to help alleviate the stress that another individual is dealing with. It is altruism: a connection to others, a sense of caring, and the drive to ease suffering. The Dalai Lama defines compassion as "an openness to the suffering of others with a commitment to relieve it." This indicates that we must be aware of suffering, feel it with empathetic concern, and respond by being involved in an act to help relieve that suffering in some way. Donating your time and energy to a cause you believe in is a form of compassion, holding the door for someone on crutches is another form of compassion, and authentically smiling at someone distressed due to life circumstances is another form of compassion. Compassion can easily be granted by being kind to others.

Along with plants, I am an animal lover and believe that the compassion we show our animals is an indicator of a person's ability to be kind to others. Many years ago, a ninth-grade student was excited to adopt a little dog. This student showed me pictures daily and would announce how many days it would take until she was able to bring the dog home. When she finally had the opportunity to bring the dog home, she was beyond ecstatic and shared photo after photo of their exploits.

Fast-forward two years. This same student is now a busy, outgoing junior. She is involved in the school's broadcast team, is involved in sports, and has a job. The little dog that she had spent so much time with at the beginning was now languishing at home in a kennel for nearly sixteen hours a day.

This student knew that her actions were unkind and irresponsible on her part and explained, while spilling tears down her face, her situation when she stopped by my class one day. I offered to help her find a new home for the dog because I couldn't imagine allowing that poor soul to continue being cooped up all day. She sent me pictures, and I emailed a plea to everyone I knew, including my husband. While some people showed a bit of interest, my husband fell in love with the picture, and we promptly went to meet my student's dog. When we arrived, our future family member jumped into my husband's lap and started licking his face. This little soul knew instinctively who her new family would be and came home with us that day.

The compassion shown in the little dog story was my student's response to the issue with her dog and my wish to help ease her plight with kindness and understanding. An added bonus? My husband and I received a new little furry family member whom I adore each day.

Empathy and Compassion

If compassion is the water for our pothos ivy, then empathy is the watering can. You can't transport water without some type of vessel to carry it in.

According to a Forbes article by Rasmus Hougaard *Four Reasons Why Compassion Is Better For Humanity Than Empathy*, empathy can be impulsive, divisive, inert, and draining (2020). Why? We mentally consider empathy tiring because we join in the suffering. Empathy can be painful, sorrowful, and gut-wrenching. Although empathy can be considered draining, it is a connection made between people, an expression of understanding, and an expression of humanness.

Compassion is similar but different. Compassion is deliberate, unifying, active, and regenerative. Compassion can put you in a state of joy and giving because of the way it can make you feel. This is an action that can be taught, and it makes one want to regularly show even greater compassion. It is the inner self, filled with a sense of self-awareness, reaching out externally with emotion to help someone or something in need.

For many years, I was an advisor for the Health Occupation Students of America (HOSA). These are students who had a deep interest in the medical field. They had regular meetings, and there was a great deal of volunteer opportunities for the members of this student-led organization.

One year, many of the students were also in a certification program (certified nurse assistant) and had spent a great deal of time training at one of the local nursing homes. Much to the students' distress, many of the patients at this nursing home were lonely, and my students felt great empathy for them. It made them sad. In an effort to alleviate the resident's loneliness, they created a card drive. Volunteers spent endless hours creating homemade cards for each of the holidays and delivered the cards to the nursing home for the residents. Both the residents and workers at the nursing home were delighted by the gifts bestowed. This group of students had been some of the most naturally compassionate people I have ever encountered. As a prosocial group, they honestly loved to help people.

Another example of enduring compassion involved a group of girls in the Environmental Club at that same school. One had learned of girls without access to feminine products in underdeveloped nations, and this caused her internal distress and concern. She approached me about making reusable pads and shipping them to organizations that provide these types of supplies across the world. This amazing group of girls collected the supplies, found students to participate, organized volunteering events, and learned how to sew (with my help) as they created these items for girls in need. By the time they were completed with this amazing project of compassion, we had nearly one hundred reusable pads ready to be distributed to those in need.

Expanding the need for compassion, chief executive officers and leaders across the globe practice regular mindfulness activities such as self-reflection and meditation to increase productivity by training the mind not to wander and to assist with focus on prioritizing tasks, building creativity, and improving relationships both personally and professionally. Meditation has been shown to boost emotional intelligence, the ability to govern emotions, and the ability to empathize with the emotions of others. This decreases anxiety and develops patience, which boosts resilience to perform under stressful conditions. Increased compassion for others occurs, which leads to better working conditions for leaders and employees alike.

All educators should take heed and follow in the footsteps of CEOs across the globe, mentally mobilizing to create a better workplace for their employees. If the upper echelons of business can use this form of mindfulness, imagine the impact it could have on students and their ability to share compassion with others.

As we discuss the effectiveness of values being included as part of the educational experience, you will learn how compassion can be taught through respecting each other and how collaboration can bring a sense of belonging to students. We will also discuss, in-depth, the importance of how tolerance, inclusion, and acceptance can manifest in a compassionate environment as connections are formed between all students in a class.

The Science of Compassion

Regularly being compassionate benefits both our physical and mental health and our overall well-being. It makes us feel good. Several studies have been performed to indicate that the prefrontal lobe and right supramarginal gyrus are active in social communication. While being compassionate to others, which requires communication, these areas activate the limbic area of the brain, which is related to reward and pleasure. In addition, feel-good chemicals such as oxytocin, dopamine, and serotonin increase in our bodies while we practice compassion.

According to the National Institutes of Health, oxytocin regulates our social behaviors by eliciting happiness, influencing feelings of trust, and helping us bond with others (Love, 2014). Dopamine release is increased in the brain and coordinates the reward centers, which brings us feelings of pleasure. Without adequate dopamine levels in the brain and bloodstream, we are unable to feel pleasure. Serotonin levels increase, which provides a feeling of euphoria and plays a large role in regulating mood. Many antidepressants on the market play on serotonin interactions in the body. These biochemicals are released and increase in our bodies as a result of making connections and maintaining a sense of belonging during compassionate moments.

Self-Compassion

Self-compassion is inwardly treating yourself as you would treat another person in need of compassion while realizing that struggle is normal and part of being human. There are three components to self-compassion: being kind and understanding to yourself instead of being self-critical; seeing one's frailty as part of the human condition and not isolating yourself from others; and being mindfully aware of the situation rather than experiencing avoidance or obsession with an issue. We are our own worst critics and tend to overthink situations that have happened in our lives. We tend to self-judge, self-critique, and self-denigrate ourselves as a habit. This is a habit that needs to be broken and reformed into a healthy ritual. Dr. Kristin Neff, an expert in the field of self-compassion, states, "Instead of mercilessly judging and criticizing yourself for various inadequacies or shortcomings, self-compassion means you are kind and understanding when confronted with personal failings—after all, who ever said you were supposed to be perfect?" (Neff, "Self-Compassion").

In addition to becoming more compassionate with others and extending this value into our daily lives, we must also extend that same hand to ourselves in the form of self-compassion. Compassion and self-compassion can be nurtured by teaching, modeling, and being an example for other people, especially your students. This value has been shown to grow with regular practice. Below are a few exercises that can help you develop a deeper level of self-awareness as you work toward a sense of increased well-being.

Modeling and Implementing Compassion Practice

As a values-imbued educator, there are many ways you can implement the practice of compassion in the classroom. The more compassion you model, the more the students will feel you have created a safe space and will want to learn in your classroom.

1. Listen actively and compassionately and be aware of the student's feelings. Actively listen to their concerns and needs.

2. Use neutral body language with eye contact. Don't cross your arms or have a defensive stance.

3. Reach out when a student has been out for more than a day or two. Let them know you are thinking about them.

4. Allow social interaction during class while students collaborate or after a lesson has been completed.

5. Give genuine, authentic praise for a job well done or an attempt at something difficult, such as when a student works outside their comfort zone.

6. Assume that students have a difficult life and treat each day as a new day. Forgive students for bad choices.

7. Create an Act of Kindness box where students can anonymously report when someone has been kind or shown compassion.

8. Prepare creative and meaningful lessons for the students that apply compassion practices. Examples include role-playing, team building, involvement in community projects, and projects that have a compassionate practice requirement.

Self-Compassion Journaling Exercise:

Answer the following questions reflectively in your journal. These questions apply to you as a person, but they can also be used in the classroom with students.

1. Think about a time when a friend was struggling. How did you respond? What did you say? What did you do?

2. Now, visualize a time when you were struggling. How did you respond to yourself?

3. What is the difference? Why? How did you self-criticize? Did you feel alone or did you feel supported by others?

4. Now, write down how you would treat yourself in that same situation if you controlled the self-critic by speaking to yourself kindly with compassion.

After answering the questions above, take a short break to reflect on what you have written. If you are working individually, add any additional notes that may have come to mind. If performing this exercise in a group, have another member of the study group share their answers as you listen without judgment, and then you do the same.

Compassion Meditation

If CEOs and leaders are using meditation to enhance their careers and experiences with employees, we should practice it with our students. What is an appropriate technique to use in the classroom?

There are many meditations available online with lovely music and verbal guidance. I have used the one below multiple times while practicing to improve my ability to be more self-compassionate and compassionate with others.

1. Close your eyes or soften your gaze down your nose.

2. Breathe gently a few times. Use rectangular breathing if you are having a hard time slowing your mind.

3. Think of someone in your life that you care about. It can be a person or even a beloved pet. Imagine that person looking directly into your eyes as you continue to breathe gently. Share your heart with this person by stating, "May you be happy, healthy, and free from fear."

4. As you continue breathing gently, think of your heart space and tell yourself, "May I be happy, healthy, and free from fear."

5. Continue breathing and visualize an acquaintance, someone you are not very close to. Tell them, "May you be happy, healthy, and free from fear."

6. Keep breathing gently and think of someone you dislike or have had issues with. Imagine that person sitting in front of you. Once again, tell this person, "May you be happy, healthy, and free from fear."

7. Breathe slowly for a few breaths as you think of your heart space.

8. Imagine the feelings from your heart filling your body, the room you are in, and the building you are in. Slowly expand this feeling until it embraces the entire planet.

9. Imagine you are on the space station looking at our planet, embraced in the feelings from your heart. Tell the people of the world, "May you be happy, healthy, and free from fear.

10. Continue breathing and end by thanking all the people you included in this meditation, including yourself.

11. As this meditation practice draws to a close, place your hand over your heart, slowly open your eyes, and smile.

Quick Self-Compassion Meditation Options:

During a frantic school day, we tend to have very little time to stop and smell the roses. Here are two moments of pause

or breathing practices you can integrate in just a few moments of the day.

1. Take a deep breath and slowly release it. Close your eyes. Notice any tension you are holding in your body and release it.

2. Sit or stand with your feet on the floor. Close your eyes and take a rectangular breath five times.

Self-Compassion and Compassion Practice Conclusion

After reading this chapter and engaging with the exercises, how do you feel about yourself as a compassionate educator? If you feel you need some work in this area, repeat the compassion meditation or look online at Dr. Kristin Neff's materials at www.self-compassion.org. Compassion and self-compassion are learned value traits that can always be improved upon.

Chapter 5 Summary

Compassion is the act of recognizing someone in need, feeling those needs within yourself, and resolving to help that person with their needs. It can be experienced in a myriad of ways, as can self-compassion. Self-compassion is being compassionate to yourself by recognizing your own needs, knowing that you are not alone in feeling these needs by not segregating yourself from others, and being mindfully aware of those needs in a nonjudgmental fashion. Compassion can be taught and nurtured within individuals through modeling and practice.

We have now planted our pothos ivy in a large, sturdy pot. We have given it healthy soil and provided ample light. With compassion, we have provided it with the right amount of water.

It now has the capacity to grow into a luscious, green organism we can feast our eyes upon!

As you continue your journey to be a values-inspired educator, you will learn about respect and self-respect and how they can be taught and enjoyed daily. Let's dive in!

"Love and compassion are necessities, not luxuries. Without them, humanity cannot survive."

Dalai Lama XIV

Chapter 6

Respectfulness

On a cool fall day, my siblings and parents met me at a bustling restaurant for brunch. As we waited for a table, the church next door had just dismissed its parishioners. As a result, a crowd filled the entryway, and the place was brimming with waiting, irate, hungry customers. After being seated, a haggardly, tired young man greeted our table, handed us menus, and hustled to the next table. I watched him apologize to an angry-looking group of customers for the delay in service, and he walked away with slumped shoulders. When the waiter reached our table, he began an apology, expecting discourteous behavior from our little group. My stepfather stopped him mid-sentence, asked his name, and thanked him for working so hard to get to our table. This took our waiter by surprise as he paused, looked at my stepfather inquisitively, and then smiled the biggest, most authentic smile I have seen in quite a while.

Respect is needed to build a better society, and it is something that should be received by all despite whatever circumstances are occurring. Just as the story above illustrates, even strangers deserve nonjudgment and unconditional respect. I'm a firm believer that all people must be respected, even if our truths do not align. I simply do not know someone else's truth unless I ask. Upon asking, respect should still be given in a nonjudgmental fashion.

Both self-respect and respect for others are the fertilizer, the needed nutrients that our pothos ivy needs to thrive and become its most glorious green self. Micronutrients such as nitrogen, phosphorus, and potassium are required for the normal growth of all plants, but other minerals such as magnesium and iron should be applied with some type of fertilizer. Unconditional real respect is a nutrient that feeds us as teachers and our students as learners. It makes each of us feel needed, wanted and appreciated. It is another source of energy that can fill our cup each day as we impart values and education.

What Is Respect?

The word respect is formed from the Latin word *respectus,* which means "to look back at," and it is an important quality in relationships. As the Golden Rule dictates "Do to others as you would have them do unto you," which means to treat others the way you want to be treated. It's not only the way you treat others but also how you treat yourself.

Just how do you treat yourself? Do you trust yourself? Do you practice self-compassion and self-reflection to build trust within yourself? Do you take the time to develop this self-awareness in order to enhance your well-being?

76

The value of respect shows how someone or something is taken seriously. It is a personalized response toward a person, place, or thing. This includes all people, nonliving objects, and the natural world. Since this book is about applying values in the classroom, we will only refer to people: the human beings living in our communities, cities, and countries on this planet.

Respect is a way of showing that you feel someone or something has value in your life. Conversely, when someone is disrespectful, it indicates a lack of belief in someone or something, and it's important to put that into proper context. A person's behavior or actions may elicit a feeling of disrespect, but not the person involved in that behavior. This reminds me of a time when a student was excessively rude to me in class by cursing at me. Unfortunately, this student routinely cursed in my presence, although not directed at me. I pulled her aside, asked her to pause and self-reflect, then asked what was going on to make her find it okay to curse at me. She said that I "failed her" and she didn't care what I thought at that moment. We then sat down with the grade book, discussed her grades, and created a battle plan to bring her up to a passing grade. I was not happy about being cursed at, but she and I came to a mutual understanding due to the mutual respect that had been earned throughout the school year. I didn't consider the behavior as who she was; it was only an aspect of her personality on that day. Only that day.

Establishing mutual trust, which leads to respect, is an important part of values education. Respect can be facilitated by treating others with kindness and dignity and by simply considering their emotions. Even though everyone has different viewpoints and truths, respect should not be withdrawn if we do not agree. Why is this important? As the teacher, it is imperative to consider why a student acts out and not personalize that behavior as the actual student. You don't have to respect their behavior, but you should show the student that he or she has value by finding out why that behavior occurred. We need to show respect to the child, not disrespect the child regardless of their behavior.

Despite my attempts to have a harmonious classroom filled with values-based lessons and curriculum, I still had a student who chose to listen to music through earphones in class. At the beginning of the year, I reminded her numerous times throughout each class period to remove her earbuds and be an active learner. After providing me with a dirty look, she would act as if she were taking them out. As soon as I turned around, she would put them back in, hiding them under her hair. I found this behavior disrespectful toward the rules and procedures of class, thus the learning environment. I didn't understand her behavior.

What did I do to find out why she continued to break the classroom rules? I respected her enough to ask her why. She explained that she had chronic ringing of the ears, and music dampened the discomfort. I allowed her to continue wearing her earphones in class as long as the volume stayed low. If I didn't have respect for her as a person, I wouldn't have asked and wouldn't have had the opportunity to be compassionate toward her and her situation.

Self-Respect

One of my girl seniors started dating another boy who was a popular football player. He showered her with attention at first, which she craved after feeling invisible for years. After a month of dating, he started to become controlling and jealous. He told the girl how to dress, who she could talk to, and that she was lucky to have him when no one else noticed her. She came to me about this issue when she felt her well-being hit rock bottom. I advised her to look into her heart and self-reflect on why she was in this predicament and sent her to her next class. I know that may seem insensitive, but she needed to take the time to self-reflect without my influence.

The next day, the football player yelled at her in the cafeteria for chatting with a male classmate. This was her breaking point, and she broke up with him. In tears, she came to my room for support. At this point, she heeded my advice and truly reflected on her situation. As a result, she discovered that she had been allowing this boy to challenge her values, and for a short period of time, she had lost respect for herself by allowing him to control her life. She had realized that she needed to show herself love and care, not endure derisive arguments with a boy who did not honestly care for her. She learned, in a difficult fashion, that respect starts within.

Respect starts with you. What does that mean? Do you practice self-respect by practicing self-compassion in order to build up that self-respect?

We all must have a healthy dose of self-respect to find our way in life. This is not egotism or narcissism. This is something you give yourself, which is fundamental to creating a mutually respectful relationship with others. Since respect builds upon itself, it is challenging to respect others when we don't respect ourselves. In return, it is difficult to respect ourselves when others don't respect us.

Respect for others and self-respect are connected. Recognizing your level of self-respect is a lifelong journey as you recognize the confidence to do what you say and follow your own set of core values. You communicate to the world that you are important when you respect yourself and that you have taken the time to recognize your skills. Unfortunately, the value of self-respect tends to be taken for granted, and thus, it is not developed by students and adults as part of increasing well-being and self-awareness.

Respecting oneself means loving yourself and treating yourself with care. It makes us less fearful of rejection or failure and more self-assured. As our self-assurance increases, this encourages us to take on new challenges and develop personally. Individual growth through self-awareness and self-confidence also makes us feel more at ease talking with others. In turn, those who care about us and respect our perspectives reciprocate our comfort level by opening their hearts and minds to us.

The Science of Respect

When you are shown respect, neurobiologists have discovered that the brain's ventral tegmental area stimulates the release of oxytocin, serotonin, and dopamine. These are feel-good chemicals that are part of your reward system. They have a multitude of physiological effects, such as relaxing the blood vessels, influencing your digestive system, and increasing your quality of sleep. In addition, they give you a feeling of optimism, motivation, and happiness.

When you feel disrespected, your body interprets this as a threat and activates your self-preservation instincts. In your brain, the amygdala is activated, which sends signals to the hypothalamus. The hypothalamus then triggers the stress response of fight, flight, or freeze, which initiates the release of chemicals such as adrenaline and cortisol. You will then experience symptoms such as an increased heart rate, rapid breathing, tense muscles, anger, and a wish to lash out.

How Do We Develop Respect in the Classroom?

Students tend to lack self-confidence and undervalue themselves. This can negatively impact their ability to form relationships and engage effectively with others. This affects their ability to be resilient and manage uncomfortable situations in life. When students are shown respect, they learn to believe in themselves, thus increasing their resilience to setbacks.

To instill respect in the classroom, we must know our personal values and model those daily, providing nutrients to our students and ourselves. This includes the language that is used. Holloman and Yates have developed a way of rephrasing our language to be positive rather than negative in the *Journal of Positive Behavior Interventions*. By being positive in word and deed, we can build a culture of respect. They identified eleven categories of words that foster respect, such as words of encouragement, guidance, high expectations, hope, sensitivity, relationship, understanding, respect, unity, and accountability (2012).

Modeling respect leads to a classroom that's based on a growth mindset. When developing a classroom based on a growth mindset, respect is gained, and effectively, a culture of respect is formed.

How does that happen?

It begins with a purposeful activity that you bring to light with your students. A growth mindset in a culture of respect offers a safe environment by encouraging effort and offering a safe place to ask for help without judgment A growth mindset in a culture of respect expresses your high expectations and accountability by positively envisioning their future with them and allowing them to pursue those goals as learners inside and outside your class.

A growth mindset and a culture of respect provide hope by helping your students see that difficulties are a part of life and that they have the talents to solve challenges. You model a culture of respect by showing that you value relationships and being sensitive and understanding by showing compassion and kindness every day. You continue to model that culture of respect as you foster a sense of unity by making sure that your students know that they belong through teamwork and collaboration.

What does this look like in the classroom? Below is a list of basic behaviors that students tend to respect. Modeling each of these behaviors will lead to a feeling of safety, a place where students want to be, and a place where they want to learn, in effect respecting you and your wish to instill a love of learning in them.

- Be on time and start class on time.
- Establish classroom expectations on day one.
- Make sure the students know all objectives to be covered and that all students can see and hear what is being discussed.
- Make eye contact with students.
- Use an approachable voice. Do not yell.
- Use students' names.
- Actively listen and provide opportunities for questions.
- Be clear and consistent.
- Praise any effort, both verbally and nonverbally.
- Be inclusive of all students.
- Be sensitive to conflicts and help to resolve them.
- Use polite language.

- Give second chances.
- Agree to disagree.
- Value dignity.

When each of the above is displayed and modeled in a classroom with students, respect is earned. Respect is earned in the eyes of your students, which stimulates their brain to release biochemicals into the brain, which makes them feel safe. Feeling safe stimulates the body to relax, which leads to an environment ripe for learning and a willingness to try new things as part of that learning process. When we, as educators, show respect, we also receive that respect.

Respect Exercise:

Answer the following questions reflectively in your journal. These questions apply to you as a person but can also be modified for use in the classroom with students.

1. Look at the listing of words below. Write in your journal about a time when you did one of these things to another person. If you could do it over again, how could you change your response to show respect? **This is deeply personal, so it is optional to share what you have written. If you do share, make sure to nonjudgmentally exchange that responsibility with someone in your group.**

Forced	Judged
Ignored	Rejected
Threatened	Did not listen to someone
Imposed upon	Manipulated

Lied	Evaded questions
Did not show care	Assumed
Mocked	Believed something was better for someone without consulting them
Stereotyped	
Underestimated	Invaded privacy
Did not take something seriously	Did not accept
Did not acknowledge needs	Betrayed
	Controlled
Did not answer a question	Laughed at

2.   Create a recipe for respect. Be creative with your ingredients. **If you are doing the exercises individually, remove this page from your journal and place it in a prominent place to remember how to "bake" respect. If you are performing this exercise in a group, share your recipe with an elbow partner or someone in the group. If you do this with your students, you can have the students display their recipes in the classroom.**

Chapter 6 Summary

All people should be afforded respect, which is a way of demonstrating that someone has value in your life. Self-respect is required to model authentic respect for others. When you show respect for yourself and your beliefs, you are able to be authentically respectful of others. When we feel respected and respect others, various biochemicals are released within our brain's internal reward system, which influences mood and balance. There are some basic actions and behaviors that show respect to students, and being consistent in these behaviors will help students show respect to you and their peers.

Our beautiful pothos ivy has a strong foundation of core values in the form of a pot and, due to the implementation of trust, healthy soil. In addition, reflection has added light, and compassion has watered it. Now, micronutrients and macronutrients have been added to the soil in the form of respect. Our little pothos ivy has begun to grow large and needs room to expand its lovely vines and leaves through the process of collaboration.

Collaboration forges a feeling of belonging in the classroom and is next on our list of values we will discuss.

"To laugh often and much;
to win the respect of intelligent people
and the affection of children;
to earn the appreciation of honest critics
and endure the betrayal of false friends;
to appreciate beauty;
to find the best in others;
to leave the world a bit better whether by a healthy child,
a garden patch, or a redeemed social condition;
to know even one life has breathed easier
because you lived.
This is to have succeeded."

Ralph Waldo Emerson

Chapter 7

Collaboration with Team Building

I recently went kayaking during a summer vacation in Florida. It was sunny and warm, fish were jumping nearby, and the water was crystal clear as we lowered the boat into the water. My father and I were in a double kayak and planned on rowing in tandem to guide ourselves through a mangrove near the shoreline. At first, we let the water lead us to the entry to the mangroves, but we soon needed to row so we wouldn't crash into the trees.

We both started to row, not connected in stroke, and ran into the approaching beach by the trees and then into the roots at the beginning of the mangrove forest. The kayak didn't know which way to turn. After a great deal of grunting and groaning, intermingled with expletives, we managed to align our oars properly and eventually maneuvered the kayak under intertwined branches into the mangroves. It was a lovely afternoon as we slowly glided through the peaceful quietness and natural beauty.

A potentially treacherous journey with my eighty-eight-year-old father became smooth and enjoyable. It took a bit of work, but we managed to collaborate and share our oar movement rhythm to achieve a goal. That goal was to enjoy peace under the mangrove in a kayak on a warm, beautiful summer day as father and daughter.

As Charles Darwin stated, "In the long history of humankind (and animal kind, too) those who learned to collaborate and improvise most effectively have prevailed." As members of a community, we are part of a greater whole, individuals who move together through life, whether we know the people around us or not. We see this collaboration daily by conscientiously taking turns at a stop sign while driving, admiring the teamwork displayed at the grocery store checkout line, or simply enjoying a meal with friends as we share day-to-day challenges. Collaboration is a delicate dance that gives us a sense of belonging as we share our skills, knowledge, time, and talents.

Collaboration is the room for the growth of our pothos ivy. It has the space to expand as it grows with self-awareness and its ability to interact with its environment as it absorbs light to create energy. Energy that is produced within the cells of the leaves and shared with stems and roots is a collaboration of the parts that make a whole. Collaboration allows us to make connections with others and find people we can interact with as we establish a sense of belonging—both in the classroom and in everyday life.

Belonging and Maslow

Early on a Saturday morning, while sipping coffee, I watched my little dog, whom I referred to in Chapter 5. She rolled around in the grass, stretched on her back, and enjoyed the sun on her belly while she looked at my husband with complete adoration. Our orange tabby cat slinked along the fence line between the potted plants and watched the dog for a chance to pounce so they could playfully roll around in the yard together. This was their ritual, and they loved it, and we loved to watch them play. They both sensed that they were cherished for who they were as members of our little family. They felt the acceptance and the value they held in our hearts; they simply knew they belonged, and they both had a sense of identity, acceptance, security, and inclusion.

Just what is *belonging*? What does a sense of belonging do for us as individuals? It's a feeling of connection, a connection both socially with other people and with physical places, such as a home, church, or school. Where a physical place of belonging and cultural belonging play a role in increased well-being, we will focus on the social aspects such as family, friends, and schoolmates. When you experience the sensation of belonging, you feel safe to be yourself, secure in your relationships, and fully included since you and your thoughts and your actions as a person within that group are valued.

According to Maslow's Hierarchy of Needs theory, our social needs fall into a third dimension—only achieved after feeling security and safety after physiological survival. Belonging is a basic desire that all people strive to fulfill because when we feel valued as human beings, there is a wish, a yearning, to develop attachments. When we develop those attachments, we make connections with others, which enhances the feeling of belonging even more. As we achieve these interpersonal relationships and feel connected, we can continue on our path to self-actualization and transcendence on Maslow's pyramid.

Collaboration and Belonging

We live in a worldwide community, and collaboration between colleagues and peers is commonly found in the workplace as a tool in business with the benefit of bringing people together. This increases the sense of belonging within an organization. The feeling of being included, accepted, respected, and knowing you are being heard within a community, whether that community is at home, school, or work, is a critical factor in positively promoting increased well-being and, thus, mental health.

At school, teachers collaborate as they share lesson plans and create inventive ways to produce student success within a curriculum stream. When teachers collaborate with two or more people, they act out the saying, "Two heads are better than one." An efficient machine is a team that bounces ideas off each other, discusses topics, and uses their knowledge to bring about engaging and meaningful lessons in the classroom. Acting as a team brings people together and increases feelings of belongingness.

In the classroom, the art of collaboration begins at an early age. Students play together at the playground, learn to share supplies, and learn how to read by reading aloud to others. As we advance in age, it becomes the activity of working in small groups to solve problems creatively by contributing to the whole group in a classroom with peers. This is a tool the students need to learn in the classroom to create a sense of belonging as they become proactive citizens in today's society, which leads to a healthier tomorrow. When we contribute as group members, we are acting as pieces of a whole; similar to pieces of a puzzle. The pieces are separate, but if diligently put together, they form a picture. This picture represents the whole, just as teams share information and learn from each other. Effective collaborative teams take the time and share their skills and talents to fashion together an intricate picture within a puzzle.

Just what does collaboration accomplish in the classroom? It encourages creative problem-solving as students brainstorm ideas and bring to light different insights regarding topics being covered in class. Students build much-needed social skills, such as active listening, as they share and include others in their conversations. This improves relationships, helps to fulfill Maslow's third dimension, enhances well-being, and can be fun for students and teachers alike.

The Science of Collaboration and Belonging

What is the science behind positive collaboration and belonging? When we feel we belong in a group, such as a collaborative team, our reward pathway in the brain is activated. Since I have referred to our feel-good biochemicals, such as oxytocin, in previous chapters, I'm going to focus on the mesolimbic pathway and the role of dopamine in this chapter.

Imagine a pleasurable experience, such as singing karaoke with friends at a club or eating a delicious meal at a newly found restaurant. Pleasurable experiences activate the ventral tegmental area (VTA) of the midbrain, which, in turn, releases dopamine. Dopamine travels along different pathways of the brain to the prefrontal cortex, the nucleus accumbens, and the hippocampus. The hippocampus is responsible for forming memories, the nucleus accumbens focuses on motor functions such as movement, and the prefrontal cortex coordinates attention and planning. As part of the dopamine secretion, we form memories associated with the pleasurable act, such as who we are with, where we are, and what we did that was enjoyable. The nucleus accumbens will facilitate the coordinated movement required, and the prefrontal cortex will pay even closer attention to the pleasurable moments being experienced. As the fun and pleasure are sustained, additional dopamine is released, forming stronger and longer-lasting memories. Singing and laughing with your friends during karaoke or enjoying that delicious meal will be remembered with fondness, and a wish to return to that time will occur in your mind long after the activities have ceased.

The same happens in our brains when we experience a sense of belonging. Therefore, we look forward to interactions of belongingness. Dopamine will be released when we enjoy moments with friends, family, and colleagues, whether we are discussing a good book during a book study, hiking in the woods with a spouse, or collaborating as a team to solve a problem. When those activities are experienced positively, there is a physiological reason for it in the brain, and we continue to crave it as we continue to make deeper connections with others.

If we feel disconnected, as if we do not belong within a social group, our brain and body act as if they are under threat. The sympathetic fight, flight, freeze pathway in the body is activated via the amygdala, anterior cingulate cortex, and insula. This leads to an increased heart rate, respiratory rate, release of adrenaline, and a feeling of threat to our survival. Long-term consequences could involve increased bodily inflammation, a compromised immune system, and decreased well-being—leading to mental health instability, such as anxiety and depression.

Belonging Journaling Exercise:

Answer the following questions reflectively in your journal. These questions apply to you as a person but can also be used in the classroom with students.

1. Think of a time when you struggled to belong in a group. List three to five words that describe how that felt.

2. Think of a time when you truly felt like you belonged to a group. List three to five words that express how that felt.

3. Reflect on the words that you wrote for numbers one and two above. Which experiences fit in with your core values that you discovered in Chapter 2?

After answering the questions above, take a short break to reflect on what you have written. If you are working individually, add any additional notes that may have come to mind. If performing this exercise in a group, have another member of the study group share their answers while you listen without judgment, and then you do the same.

Why I Love Student Collaboration

A group of students wearing lab aprons, goggles, and gloves leans close to the heart specimen on their lab station. They have been tasked with finding the great vessels that leave and enter the heart with probes and locate the valves associated with each artery and vein. Due to biological individuality and the way the hearts were stored during preservation, the specimens don't look like the drawings displayed in the front of the classroom.

At one of the lab stations, students are struggling to find the vessels and pass the heart around as they brainstorm where the probes should go. At another station, the students have located the great vessels, inserted the probes, and are discussing valve location. Another station has a group of bilingual students discussing in Spanish what valves they are to locate and how to find them.

Each collaborative group is deep in discussion and learning from each other. They share their knowledge, demonstrate their skills, and problem-solve as an integrated team. Each student is highly engaged and is developing a deep sense of connection with their group members.

As Aristotle stated, "The whole is greater than the sum of its parts." Thus, a proactive, collaborative assignment includes students being active and taking ownership and responsibility for their part in the activity. These collaborative exercises in class establish your high expectations as a teacher, and the students demonstrate values such as trust, respect, and belonging as part of a collaborative group.

Values and Collaboration

How can this be used to bring about peaceful learning experiences that develop a sense of belonging and an increased sense of well-being as part of collaboration? At the beginning of each year, I use team-building exercises so that we all get to know each other. The first two weeks are mostly collaboration exercises as the students learn the rules, procedures, and expectations required in my classroom. Many ideas for team building can be found online, which is where I found the ones listed below. I am providing my version of these because they are quick, easily set up, and great fun for all.

1. **Marshmallow Spaghetti Tower**. Teams build the tallest free-standing structure with twenty pieces of spaghetti, one meter of masking tape, and one large marshmallow. Teams have fifteen minutes to build the largest tower they can in comparison to the other teams in the classroom. After the competition and recognition of the largest tower, we debrief with questions such as:

   a. Did someone emerge as a leader in your group?

   b. Could you have accomplished this task without a leader?

   c. Was everyone in the group involved?

   d. What could have been done differently?

   e. Did you celebrate small wins?

2. **Beach Ball Toss**. I have random questions written on a beach ball, such as "What's your favorite holiday?" "Sweet or Salty?" "What's your favorite show to binge-watch?" Students form a circle and randomly throw the ball around the circle. Each student answers a question that is closest to their right thumb as they catch the ball. This activity allows the students to learn similarities and future connections that can be made between each other.

3. **Helium Stick.** I use an eight-foot-long piece of bamboo for this activity. Students line up in two rows, facing each other. Everyone puts their arms straight out and sticks out their pointer finger. I then place the stick on their pointed fingers. The group is to lower the helium stick to the ground while all fingers remain in contact with the stick. After the activity has concluded, we debrief with questions such as:

   a. What did the stick do at first?

95

b. Why do you think this happened?

c. What creative solutions were suggested, and how were they received?

d. What were your strengths? Weaknesses?

As the year progresses and content is learned, students are placed into collaborative groups to perform labs, assess case studies, solve puzzles, perform jigsaw activities, and play competitive games. My favorite is Problem-Based Learning. I give students a problem with very little introduction, and they create a solution as a collaborative team. Many examples are discussed in my first book, *My Teachable Moments,* such as growing lettuce in groups, sprouting pinto beans, and creating water filtration devices. You can get a copy of the book at ww.docmcpherson.com.

One of my favorites that was not discussed in *My Teachable Moments* was having students use common and random objects to create a digestive system. They would use items such as plastic baggies, balloons, rubber bands, and plastic cups to create a working model of the digestive system. Their goal was to learn about the organs of a healthy digestive system and have their prototype chew and digest a piece of bread with a small amount of water. All activities, such as chewing, peristalsis, and digestion, were to be demonstrated. It was frustrating for them at first because testing was messy, and the first few attempts didn't work. Generally, each group had to go back to the drawing board multiple times. There was always plenty of grunting and groaning as they eventually prevailed as a cohesive, collaborative team. When the students presented their projects, I tied the curriculum together by asking questions about diseases that affect each aspect of their project as food makes its way through the body system.

These students learned much more than I could have ever taught them as their teacher. They learned to contribute authentic ideas, focused on critical thinking, and involved each team member as they built social connections and developed a sense of belonging as they shared ideas and fostered a community that supported each other.

Ideas for Collaboration

Teamwork and collaboration as a learning tool can be used at any age. Depending on the age of the learner, it is a good idea to discuss and monitor expectations, such as the roles each student will play, in order for the collaborative experience to be beneficial in establishing a sense of inclusion and belonging. Here's a list that I've used with great success throughout the years:

1. **Think-pair-share**. The teacher poses a question, and students write down an answer or their thoughts for one minute, pair with a partner, and then share what they wrote with each other for one minute.

2. **Brainwriting**. Brainstorming is a great tool, but generally, the fastest or the loudest tends to take over the conversation. To avoid this issue, have team members write their ideas down on sticky notes or in a notebook, then discuss each idea in turn. An alternative is to have each brainstormed idea written on a sticky note and posted on the walls, then have the class vote on their favorite ideas.

3. **Art projects**. Some of the most amazing art I've seen has been completed in small collaborative groups. Each student focuses on their specific talent. Examples have been creating fractured bones with clay, creating cell models with salt

dough, and drawing full-sized bodies on large paper. I discuss this activity and provide a picture of a full-sized skeleton in *My Teachable Moments*.

4. **Games using technology.** There are a multitude of gaming options that teachers can use for free online. If students compete as teams, it actually adds a competitive vibe to collaborative teams as groups rush to answer review questions.

5. **Role-playing or performing a dramatic skit.** This can be great fun to discuss a wide variety of topics.

Chapter 7 Summary

Collaboration is teamwork using higher-order thinking skills to solve a problem. As part of this engaging process, students build connections with each other as they share their time, talent, and skills. This experience instills a sense of belonging—belonging with a group that builds a whole, just as pieces of a puzzle create a picture when placed accordingly. This can help fulfill Maslow's third social dimension of belonging and establish a positive feeling of well-being.

A full range of physiological effects can be felt as the reward centers of the brain reinforce the *feel-goodness* of belonging. Teamwork activities are an effective tool to build community in the classroom, and regular collaboration throughout the school year fosters good memories as a love of learning is enhanced.

We have now established our pothos ivy within a good pot in the form of core values, given it soil in the form of unconditional trust, and provided light in the form of looking within—reflection. We have also provided ample water in the form of compassion and fed it healthy nutrients in the form of respect.

Now, we have given it room for growth so that it can interact with its environment in the form of collaboration. Our pothos ivy is growing tolerant to its environment and developing resiliency to fluctuations that may not be conducive to its growth as an attractive, dazzling entity.

Let's discover how the ongoing endeavor of tolerance can be fostered as part of values-imparted education.

**"Humankind has not woven the web of life.
We are but one thread within it.
Whatever we do to the web, we do to ourselves.
All things are bound together.
All things connect."**

Chief Seattle, 1854

Chapter 8

Tolerance to Inclusion

After getting married and moving to a different city, I was hired to teach in a suburban school district. It was 2011, the year many teachers lost their jobs, and I was thrilled to be offered a position. At the teacher in-service before the school year began, I was flabbergasted at the number of blondes and light-skinned people I would be working with. I wasn't accustomed to the lack of racial diversity, and it was a bit of a culture shock to me. I had always worked at racially diverse schools—faculty and student body included. I'm not sure if it was the community, the individuals who had been applying, or hiring practices, but it was an eye-opening experience.

While at that school, there may have been a low occurrence of racial diversity regarding black students, but there were many other shades of skin, and diversity was prevalent in different ways. We had a very open LGBQT+ (lesbian, gay, bisexual, queer, transgender) community, a wide variety of religions, many cultures from across the planet, disabled students, and students with special abilities. What I found at this school was that there was a great deal of tolerance and inclusion for individuals who would have been seen as "different" elsewhere, and it was a lovely experience. You see, many of these students had been attending school together since they were in elementary school, so this was their community of people that they related to with ease. It was natural, and it was a community of tolerance, inclusion, and acceptance.

Sesil Pir, author of "Reclaiming Our Space: Why We Need to Move From Tolerance To Acceptance For Inclusion," writes, "For years and years, the inequality, the injustice, the systemic violence, and oppression we have turned our faces from in the workplace and beyond has traumatized the deepest parts of our beings" (2021). She is correct, and it is our duty as responsible and value-conscious educators to incorporate this fact into our classrooms. Many generations have been calling for diversity and tolerance in a deep, resounding voice throughout our country and the world. As experts in our field of education, we can play a role in changing the mindsets of the old into concrete change by teaching and modeling tolerance, inclusivity, and acceptance daily in the classroom.

Our pothos ivy is growing nicely, and now is the time for maintenance to help it grow to its fullest potential. Its growth has been sustained by our values and the implementation of values-based activities, and now we must modify the external environment. Just like tolerance, inclusion, and acceptance in the classroom, temperature is also important. A pothos ivy can survive a wide range of temperatures, but it prefers between 60 and 85 degrees Fahrenheit. If the temperature becomes too cold, it stops growing, and I know from personal experience that freezing temperatures will kill it. Too hot is the same, but it tends to go dormant in the heat. If the temperature is not monitored, just as tolerance levels in your classroom, it will not prosper.

What Is Tolerance?

Tolerance is valuing and respecting a person's humanness above any beliefs, ideals, or behaviors they may have. It is the suggestion that we are all related and can respect and value differences between each other without judgment. The commonality between all people is that we are all united by our humanity, and we must learn to work together in harmony, which is difficult based on bias, societal behaviors, upbringing, and our lifetimes of experiences.

Tolerance leads to another value, which is inclusion. This is the acknowledgment of differences between people and forms a welcoming, positive atmosphere for all. We can learn to recognize those who have been excluded and actively work to include all races, cultures, beliefs, and people as valuable assets within a school and a classroom. This can lead to belonging, a subject covered extensively in Chapter 7.

While tolerance may allow prejudices and biases to be in place, it is not considered outwardly visible. It is more of an agreement to disagree without obvious stances of judgment and exclusion. Inclusion and acceptance can bypass tolerance by being more comprehensive, multiculturally sensitive, and involving those who have had a wide variety of unfair situations motivated by bias. The term inclusion refers to historically excluded individuals being included in activities such as decision-making, problem-solving, and building better communities. Acceptance is an even deeper level of tolerance and inclusion because it includes a sense of belonging. It gives permission to be oneself. Acceptance is feeling free from judgment and the understanding that others accept you for who you are, inside and out, which leads to a higher level of well-being.

Mental Health

Being included and accepted has a much higher chance of increasing a student's well-being, thus improving mental health. This applies to all cultures, races, belief systems, and sexual orientations.

The population of open LGBTQ+ students has increased over the past few decades, stimulating a need for social acceptance, but it has run into a multitude of societal barriers, such as misunderstandings, unconscious bias, and rigid thinking. Mental health statistics are staggering, according to the NIH. Thirty-nine percent of LGBTQ+ people struggle with depression, thirty-three percent endure anxiety, and twenty-eight percent have experienced suicidal ideation. These mental health issues have been found to be a result of family neglect, decreased social connection, bullying, discrimination, bias, and victimization (Moagi et al., 2021). In response, the Gay-Straight Alliance (GSA) has developed a program to empower students to build partnerships with allied students within the school walls. The GSA is a student-led, school-based club with strong ties throughout the nation that has traditionally been a safe space for students and allied youth. This program has been shown to improve the school climate toward diverse youth.

Research on religious discrimination and mental health effects is limited in scope. Bullying and intimidation tactics, along with bias, have been reported by multiple health organizations, but an appreciable amount of statistical data has not been collected. It has been assumed that religious affiliation has acted as a buffer or coping mechanism concerning mental health. It appears that religious exclusion has correlated with racial discrimination in the population of BIPOC (Black, Indigenous, and people of color).

Although BIPOC individuals, such as Hispanics and Blacks, may have similar rates of mental health disorders as non-BIPOC populations, it is considered more persistent in Blacks and Hispanics, and there is reason to believe that it may be underdiagnosed due to health care bias and stereotyping. Native and Indigenous American adults have the highest reported rate of mental illnesses, as well as a significant amount of post-traumatic stress and alcohol dependence. All BIPOC populations have had to deal with systemic racism due to exclusionary provisions set in place throughout the years. These policies include a vast arsenal of systemic discrimination, such as economic, educational, and housing. Although there has been a great deal of research and laws put in place, these issues persist and continue to lead to a disproportionate number of individuals suffering through discrimination, bias, and stereotyping.

Inclusion-Exclusion

I noticed open racist and exclusionary statements being made during the recent political cycles, so I decided it was important to discover and heal my conscious and unconscious biases. As I explored my thoughts and actions in an effort to increase self-awareness, I did quite a bit of reading and self-reflection. One such book is called *Radical Inclusion* by David Moinina Sengeh. Through his personal experiences, he provides steps to create a more inclusive world. He states in this book, "The inclusion-exclusion border is fluid. No one is on one side of it at all times; but across domains, some people are more often excluded than others" (2024). I find this very true because we are either included or not included. His first step states that we must find the exclusion and relate to that exclusion in a personal way. Do you remember a time when you were invited and included? How did it make you feel? How about when you weren't invited and included as part of an activity or something you wanted to be a part of?

In the previous chapters, we have discussed trust, reflection, compassion, respect, and collaboration, and we have looked internally as we have self-discovered our inner world. As in our previous chapters, it is important to do the same and find out where you lie in reference to the inclusion and exclusion of others. Determining biases, whether conscious or unconscious, reflecting on how we treat others we perceive as different, and learning how to bring students together are all part of the process of becoming an effective values-instilling educator.

Conscious biases are open, and we are aware of them, so they may be easier to rectify. These types of biases are intentional, such as not hiring someone due to race, gender, or age. Many laws have been enacted and are enforced by the Equal Employment Opportunity Commission. Examples of laws are Title VII of the Civil Rights Act of 1964, which protects Americans from issues such as racial and gender discrimination, and Title I of the Americans with Disabilities Act of 1990, which protects Americans with disabilities.

Subconscious biases can be more subtle, and we may not be aware of how our background and personal experiences affect the way we treat others. Our truth, as discussed in Chapter 3, may be very different from others, and we treat other people without honor or by using microaggressive language.

Our belief system dictates how the traits of others trigger our behavior, which leads to who is included and who is excluded.

This may be steeped in our traditions and learned behaviors, and we as individuals must determine if a group's beliefs that we adhere to belong to ourselves or are part of group dynamics that do not serve a higher purpose. That higher purpose is tolerance, inclusion, and acceptance.

To look within through self-reflection can be an uncomfortable process, but we must be willing to spend the time and make the effort if we are to help our students recognize and overcome their biases so that they can be proactive members of society.

Since this is a difficult process, we must remember the lessons taught in Chapter 5, "Compassion." When looking within, we must be compassionate with ourselves, we must be gentle and realize that our weaknesses are due to our humanness and that we need to relax in nonjudgment of our past beliefs and actions.

Tolerance, inclusion, and acceptance were difficult for a male student I taught many years ago. I assigned a collaborative exercise where students were to research a country as part of a Mock United Nations program in coordination with other schools in our district. We had planned to have Mock UN exercises at the end of the school year to discuss climate change and energy solutions, and each group was required to research an assigned country and represent that country to the best of their ability. We spent about a month researching and preparing for this exercise with cultural potluck meals that represented their countries, in-depth discussions about the issues of each country, and creative problem-solving sessions where solutions were brainstormed.

There was one pair of boys in this class who would not do the work assigned for their country. They completely refused to research any country that was not Anglo-Saxon in origin. I was completely aghast at their refusal and acceptance of failing this assignment because of their beliefs. After a phone call to their parents, I discovered that the apple didn't fall far from the tree, and I needed to reassign these students due to their deep-seated racial bias, which extended through multiple generations. As these young men are now adults, I hope that they have changed their viewpoints and have realized their biases regarding the rainbow of races, cultures, and diversity our beautiful planet beholds.

Self-awareness is liberating. If we take the time to see how our worldview is shaped, we can make adjustments that make the world a better place, for ourselves, our students, and our community as a whole.

Tolerance Exercises:

Answer the following questions reflectively in your journal. These questions apply to you as a person but can also be used in the classroom with students.

1.   How are you color-blind to the hue of someone's skin?

2.   How comfortable do you feel discussing prejudicial issues with others? When do you fear appearing biased?

3.   How do you honor diversity in your daily life? When do you consider feedback from others? When do you dismiss feedback from others?

4.   When have you demonstrated bias in the past? Did you recognize it at the time, or was it something you realized later? What prompted that later realization?

After answering the questions above, take a short break to reflect on what you have written. If you are working

individually, add any additional notes that may have come to mind. If performing this exercise in a group, have another member of the study group share their answers as you listen without judgment, and then you do the same.

Tolerance Exercise Conclusion

How did the questions make you feel? What part made you a bit uncomfortable? They made me uncomfortable when I first spent time in self-reflection on this subject.

I know that in the past, I had always considered myself color-blind to BIPOC, but I've learned through reading and researching that being color-blind is a racist viewpoint. I was shocked when I learned this. I honestly thought that color-blindness was the best way to end discrimination, but it was treating people as equals without regard to race, culture, or ethnicity. It was a very uncomfortable realization to learn that a color-blind approach allowed me to deny cultural differences because I chose not to see the racial disparities and inequities associated with a history of trauma and abuse. As David Moinina Sengeh states in *Radical Inclusion,* "It is possible to make positive change – if we have the facts we need and the will to do so" (2024).

I now openly engage with others in conversations about diversity, equity, and inclusion. After practice, I'm much more comfortable seeing, discussing, and dealing with my own unconscious biases when they are brought to my attention.

On a side note, there is an amazing website that has a vast number of questionnaires regarding implicit bias. https://implicit.harvard.edu/implicit/takeatest.html. I suggest you go to it and take several tests. It was truly eye-opening for me.

Exercises to Use as a Group and with Students

1. Circle of Trust: this is my variation of a popular exercise. You can find different versions of it online.

   a. Each person should write down the names of ten people that they feel they can trust who aren't related to them.

   b. Classify by placing a tick mark next to each of the trusted people. Include the following classifications: age, gender, native language, education, race/ethnicity, and sexual orientation.

   c. Each person reviews their list and discusses their list of trusted people. Most participants will find that the list includes very little diversity and is an aha moment waiting to happen.

2. Place a picture of something of interest on the screen in front of the class. Give the class five minutes to write down everything they see, feel, and interpret about that picture. Have students share what they have written down and point out the different viewpoints of the students in the class.

3. Game of Sticky Notes

   a. Place different colors and shapes of sticky notes on the front of the participants.

   b. Without specific instructions, tell the participants to form groups without talking.

   c. Once they form their groups, tell them to move into different groups.

d. Once again, have the participants move to another group.

e. Discuss how the groups were formed. Did anyone look past the sticky notes? This is a great way to explore the diversity found in the room and recognize the differences and similarities of the people in attendance.

4. Cultural Food Day. In many of my classes, we would have a day when everyone would bring in one of their family's traditional food items to share with the class. I included it as part of the curriculum during lessons on the digestive and food systems or as a "getting to know you" exercise. It was always a fun day when the students could share their heritage with great pride. In addition, I had them provide a recipe card, and I created a recipe book of the different foods shared.

Each of the above activities helps to embrace the differences between the students and opens a dialogue that engages the students as they learn tolerance, inclusion, and acceptance for their classmates, which can lead to a sense of belonging as they create trusting relationships. Our job as values-encompassing educators is, as Tehia Starker Glass, Ph.D. and Lucretia Carter Berry, Ph.D. state in *Teaching for Justice and Belonging*, "Teaching for Justice requires us to actively overcome barriers so that every child has the opportunity to be seen, safe, valued, and inspired" (2022).

Chapter 8 Summary

Tolerance is the act of valuing and respecting a person's being, their humanness, and all other aspects of their personality. Where tolerance bypasses differences between individuals,

111

inclusion allows trust to grow with a sense of belonging, which leads to acceptance within a group. Disparities in the way people are treated due to their differences have been shown to have a deleterious effect on the mental health of those who are discriminated against. We are all included and excluded at different times in our lives, and we must look within to see why we exclude others. Is it due to a bias that is conscious or unconscious? When we, as values-inclusive educators, self-reflect on our own biases and learn to communicate our differences, we can help our students become tolerant, inclusive, and accepting.

Our pothos ivy has now grown tremendously. Its leaves are reaching across the desk and flowing toward the floor. Its majestic greenness has grown with knowledge of values in its foundational pot—a feeling of trust due to healthy soil, reflection as appropriate lighting, compassion as ample water, respect as healthy nutrients in the form of fertilizer, collaboration as room to grow, and now it feels tolerance, inclusion, and acceptance with the right temperature for satisfying its ample growth. To continue amazing growth, more maintenance is needed, including the cleaning of dust from its leaves in the form of connections.

A discussion of connections and the importance of making connections is what we will delve into in the next chapter.

"Alone we can do so little; together we can do so much."

Helen Keller

Chapter 9

Making Real Connections

When I was growing up, I had difficulty feeling that I could fit in. I felt different than most of my peers and appeared shy and reclusive. In the cafeteria, I would keep to myself, and in the playground, I was often immersed in a book. I would look over the pages of the book and watch my peers chase each other around during recess and play games together in class. I didn't feel like an outcast; I just felt different. I didn't see that they had the same yearnings for knowledge as I felt. Deep down inside, I was bursting with curiosity and a wish to learn as much as possible, and the other students my age didn't appear to have such a need.

In fourth grade, an amazing teacher came along, swept me off my feet, and referred me for Gifted and Talented testing. I was accepted into the program and continued my elementary education at a school in a different part of town. This was a school where I felt I could connect with my peers. I was accepted for who I was and began to make friends at this new school. I

113

learned to love spending time with like-minded peers, whether it was solving problems together or learning something new. We bonded, and it was a new experience for me—an experience I still value as an adult.

In middle school, with the same peer group as I had in elementary school, I learned to branch out as I discovered a love of science, and I associated with others who enjoyed science as much as I did. I was making new friends and connections—ones that I had a commonality with. I loved my classes and the peers that I made connections with.

Then BOOM, high school. I was in a new school with new people. The shyness of my personality peaked its unwelcome head into my life again. I was fearful I wouldn't fit in with the groups of students I now went to school with and hid within the pages of books.

One day, a wonderful girl asked about the book I was reading. She was a junior, and I was a freshman, but that didn't stop us from discovering that our likes and dislikes were similar. She was far from shy and had a large circle of friends whom she introduced me to.

I crawled out of my self-made shell and started to make connections in this whole new world of high school. Once again, I loved being part of a group of like-minded people. We went to dances together, read books together, wrote poetry together, and did what teenagers do when they have made healthy connections; we explored life together. It felt good. I felt acceptance, and my emotional well-being was enhanced.

Our pothos ivy has grown nicely and is now in need of some additional maintenance in the form of gently cleaning the leaves.

This is important for any indoor houseplant because dust will land on the leaves, which impedes wavelengths of light from entering the cells of the plant, thus interrupting the process of photosynthesis. Photosynthesis is how plants make their food for energy. Plant leaves do need to be dusted with a damp towel or washcloth periodically. Creating and maintaining connections is equivalent to the metaphor being used in this book because cleaning the leaves is a form of maintenance. This maintenance would not be necessary without establishing some form of connection between two different things.

What Is a Connection?

A connection is the act of bringing two things together to form meaningful relationships between different people, places, or things. Humans are a social species and enjoy forming bonds through shared experiences. These experiences can be simple or complex and bring about a social connection between members of a group. Simple, such as watching a television show together, or complex, such as performing in an orchestra ensemble. For example, there's a lovely restaurant on a hillside that I used to frequent during sunsets because, at sunset, everyone would stand up and clap as the sun slid below the horizon. The appreciation and beauty of that moment would cause smiles, laughter, and a deep appreciation for nature and its beauty. Everyone in that restaurant would share that experience at the same time, and we would form a connection with each other, even though we didn't know each other outside of that moment.

According to Erikson's stages of psychosocial development, there are important milestones we traverse from birth until old age. Should we navigate each stage well, we can develop something he referred to as ego quality, another term for

115

resiliency—the ability to cope with stress and deal with adversity. As our ability to be resilient expands, our emotional intelligence—the capacity to use emotions effectively—also grows. We learn to be more competent while dealing with challenges. We can be more effective at solving our problems, and we can interact more easily with others in a more kind and meaningful way.

During infancy, we discover trust with an outcome of hope as we develop trust based on the display of showing care, affection, and the needs for survival, such as food. As experienced during early childhood, we discover our need for autonomy and will, and we develop independence as we traipse through life and develop the ability to control body systems. As preschoolers, we develop initiative and purpose as we learn that we can control the world through play. During our school-age years, we develop confidence and industry, and we develop a sense of pride as we learn new abilities and achieve school-year milestones. Adolescence leads to a sense of personal identity, which includes beliefs and values that guide someone's behavior, perhaps for the rest of their life.

Once we get past the more turbulent and angsty years of adolescence, we enter young adulthood, middle adulthood, and maturity. These focus on relationship building and forming a more pervasive personal identity, actions during work and parenthood that will benefit future generations, and at the final stage of life, we reflect on our lives as we develop wisdom.

Connections are built throughout life, and the ability to form those attachments can affect our lives in a profound way. We can either have deep, empathetic connections based on love and kindness, or we can have limited connections that isolate and decrease the fulfillment of life experiences.

Classroom Connections

There is a difference between making connections in the classroom on a social level and making connections between content and the real world. I am going to briefly touch on making real-world connections in this section.

Real-world connections are also known as experiential learning, where actual experiences occur or correlate the information learned into something more concrete. Some subjects in the classroom can be abstract and difficult to understand because you can't touch or feel the material being covered. This is why chemistry and physics tend to be perceived as difficult. It is difficult, at best, to touch and feel the nuances of these profound subjects. Teachers must be creative in these instances to bring about an understanding of the material in a real way, but it doesn't have to be difficult. It can be simply to introduce an industry-based news article into the lecture, which can turn that potentially dull lecture into a bond-building experience through discussion. Real-world connection-making can also be more detailed, such as building roller coasters in physics or cooking in chemistry.

As part of keeping students engaged in class through real-world connections, you can also enhance the process of making personal social connections for students. Students enjoy being active in the classroom and form lifelong memories as they have meaningful learning moments. This can be done by using their hands in the form of some type of manipulative, drawing cartoons that represent what's being taught, conducting laboratory activities, answering questions as a group after watching a video or reflecting on current events. The choices for hands-on learning are innumerable. As you guide your students through these real-world, and hands-on experiences, you make connections with them. You form bonds based on shared experiences, and you enjoy the experience together.

The Importance of Connection

I think of a connection between people, places, and things as a spider web. If you wiggle one strand of a spider web, the entire structure shifts and moves, much to the chagrin of the spider that built it. To me, a spider web represents a connection of all people in unity—unity in thought, belonging, and acceptance. Each thread is intertwined with another thread as the entire construction starts small and is weaved together in a concentric pattern. This is similar to the designs weaved together to form a quilt; the perceptions of many are blended as they are intricately woven together to form a larger vision.

In this book and in my classroom, the spider web and quilt represent a vision of the integration of values. These values will help create students who will apply their recognized values as skills learned. This will ripple outward into society and communities abroad.

I strive to keep my students engaged in the classroom and this requires a connection to be formed between teacher and student, which is equally as important as the connection of student to student. Engagement refers to a student's connection to how they are interacting with the content, what they are doing to learn, and who they are learning from or with. This is one reason I enjoy collaborative learning. Their connections grow by leaps and bounds when you let them figure out how to work together autonomously.

This reminds me of Schopenhauer's parable. His story is about connection and the struggle to find the balance between connection and individuality, something we all struggle with, not just our students.

"One cold winter's day, a number of porcupines huddled together quite closely in order, through their mutual warmth, to prevent themselves from being frozen. But they soon felt the effect of their quills on one another, which made them again move apart. Now, when the need for warmth once more brought them together, the drawback of the quills was repeated so that they were tossed between two evils until they had discovered the proper distance from which they could best tolerate one another. Thus, the need for society, which springs from the emptiness and monotony of men's lives, drives them together; but their many unpleasant and repulsive qualities and insufferable drawbacks once more drive them apart. The mean distance which they finally discover, and which enables them to endure being together [means] that the need for mutual warmth will be only imperfectly satisfied, but on the other hand, the prick of the quills will not be felt" (2007 edition.)

Forming connections requires a balance between people to not interrupt someone's individuality. Just as the quills on the porcupines, we must learn how to connect without losing our freewill in that relationship.

The Science of Connection

We are hardwired to form connections as social human beings. We enjoy forming social constructs, which are groups of people that come together to connect. As part of that desire to form connections, our brain has developed the ability to perceive cues, determine if those social cues are important, and predict how to appropriately respond.

Emotions are important in our attempts to make connections with each other. Brain research has determined that our emotions are not in one specific area of the brain; they are scattered throughout the gray and white matter. For instance, the amygdala has been found to be active when we are scared or fearful; disgust is found as part of the insula, and the orbitofrontal cortex recognizes rewarding social signals.

As I have discussed, I employ many collaborative activities, such as laboratory activities, in my classroom. Unfortunately, many of my students like to taste or lick what we're working with, and this always forms an emotional response from me and the other students. The first step that would occur in my brain is to recognize the student using my fusiform gyrus. After facial recognition, the insula would be activated, which would coordinate with the amygdala due to fear of the student's health outcome if they ingested the material they were licking. At the same time, the prefrontal cortex would determine a proper response and coordinate my mouth and vocal folds to respond to the behavior with "Yuck, Stop!" I'm sure the orbitofrontal cortex of students was activated as many of the students laughed crazily when they saw what was happening and my reaction.

This is a simplistic explanation of what happens in the brain, but it is still quite amazing that all of this happens in an instant.

When we are making connections, in addition to what was described above, our brain is enjoying a bath of our feel-good biochemicals such as oxytocin, serotonin, and dopamine. Once again, the reward centers of the brain are activated, which leads to a positive memory of experiencing attachment and inclusion because we have receptive people to form connections with.

Self-Connection

As in many of the chapters, we are now going to delve into self-awareness and determine our level of self-connection. How aware are we of ourselves? Do we accept ourselves? Is our behavior toward ourselves and others aligned with how we feel about ourselves?

Being connected to yourself is a form of introspection. Through self-reflection, you can determine who you are and what you stand for. We have already performed a variation of self-connection when we reflected on our core values. But how do you use those values, and are you aligning your behavior to function along with those values?

Self-connection is important because it helps us understand and increase our emotional quotient by helping us understand our emotional needs, thus making wiser decisions in everyday life. We become more self-aware as we identify areas of our lives that cause stress and anxiety. We can determine what we put our energy and attention into and whether it serves us to continue that behavior. We develop better self-acceptance to recognize our boundaries and increase our self-confidence. All in all, we can develop a greater sense of peace, which leads to increased resilience to setbacks.

Self-Connection Exercise:

Answer the following questions reflectively in your journal. These questions apply to you as a person but can also be modified for use in the classroom with students.

1. When was the last time you tried something for the first time? How did it make you feel?

2. What would you do if you knew you couldn't fail?

3. How are you living true to yourself?

4. What aspects indicate you feel you have a deep understanding of yourself?

5. What is your biggest strength?

6. What is your biggest weakness?

After answering the questions above, take a short break to reflect on what you have written. If you are working individually, add any additional notes that may have come to mind. If performing this exercise in a group, have another member of the study group share their answers as you listen without judgment, and then you do the same.

Self-Connection Exercise Conclusion

How did the questions make you feel? Were you honestly comfortable answering the questions, or did they cause some level of discomfort?

We have discussed various types of "self" values and how to interpret their meanings, and they are very similar; I have to agree. Self-connection is an evaluation of how you feel about yourself, but this cannot be fully completed without understanding your level of self-trust and your ability to self-reflect. Each is similar in that they are not self-indulgent, they are not narcissistic, and they are not for the faint of heart. It takes a deep level of commitment to look within and share that knowledge truthfully and honestly with yourself and those around you.

Student Connection Exercises:

The best way to gauge your connection with students is to observe interactions in the classroom. This can be difficult at times, and we would like more concrete answers to this quandary. I like objective evidence to coordinate with the subjective evidence collected. Here are some questionnaire-style questions you can ask the students: I've used these as a final question to conclude class, part of a reflective questionnaire online, and variations of these questions as an exit ticket.

1. Share a memorable moment from our class when you were connected to the material.

2. How do you relate to me as your teacher?

3. What would you like to see more of in our class?

4. How was there a sense of connection and community evident within this class? What is important to you about connection and community within our class?

5. How do you think we can strengthen our connection as a class moving forward?

6. What helps you feel more connected and willing to share your perspectives?

Social Connections

Earlier in this chapter, I talked about a new friend group I made in high school. After meeting the new people, I still felt worried that this new group felt sorry for the quiet little ninth grader because most of them had been friends for several years. Deep

123

down inside, it seemed as if the relationships were at a surface level and not as deep as I wanted. I was still quite shy, and I wasn't sure how to make this happen . . . to make connections.

This was in the 1980s, during the time of big hair and parachute pants and there was a song that was quite popular on the radio at the time titled "We Are the World." It included a plethora of famous musical stars raising relief money for the famine in Ethiopia, and I had admitted that I loved the song at the time to one of the girls in my new friend group.

The next day, when getting on the school bus, one of the boys in this new friend group stood up and motioned for me to sit in the back of the bus with them. One of the girls turned on her portable tape recorder and started singing "We Are the World". I joined in. We all swayed to the rhythm, and I felt like I had made a true new batch of friends. We had certainly formed a relationship, and it felt wonderful to be included and accepted as a member of their friend group.

Why do I bring up this story? Prior to making these new friends, I felt isolated from other people at this school. I simply didn't feel like I fit in, and I was beginning to feel despondent and depressed. When this group took me under their wing, I was able to escape those feelings as I was accepted as one of their own. This is no different from the students we currently have in our classrooms since they can also feel unconnected, sad, and unincluded.

As educators, you can't make students become friends, but you can include them as part of collaborative teams and stimulate connections between students in a variety of ways—many have already been mentioned in this book. Teamwork exercises at the beginning of the year and interspersed throughout the year are quite effective tools not just to build inclusion and belonging but to build connections at random times of the year. A few I used in the past are listed below:

1. **Pair and Group Stand**. Pairs sit back-to-back, arms linked. They are to try to stand up together. After they have figured out the technique, increase the number of students involved to four and six. As the number increases, they will find it is easier. The laughter is usually contagious.

2. **This and That**. This takes some preparation work on your end as you create pairs of cards such as salt and paper, peanut butter and jelly, and yin and yang. Write one of each pair on different cards. When the students enter the class, tape the card facing out on the back of each student (make sure they can't see the word on his/her back). The students are then instructed to wander around the class and ask questions until they find their partner. Once they find their partner card, they are to chat with each other while the rest of the class finds their partners.

3. **Friendship Friday**. On Fridays, the students are to get out of their chairs, find someone they don't usually partner with, and share one thing they like about themselves and one thing they like about the person they are talking with. This is a positive validation exercise that makes everyone feel good.

Chapter 9 Summary

Connections are developed when two things are brought together. In this case, people are being brought together to develop meaningful relationships and to develop a sense of belonging. As we develop connections, we become more resilient to setbacks and emerge with a greater sense of well-being. Connections in the classroom are made through engagement, both with the teacher and with students. This is confirmed by brain science as emotions in relation to interactions with others have been studied. In addition to understanding connections as a process with others, we also have self-connection to consider. Our self-awareness can be enhanced as we search within ourselves to see if we are unequivocally connected.

Our lovely pothos ivy has grown beautifully with cascading leaves that fall gracefully along the front of our desk. A strong foundation of values, trust, reflection, compassion, respect, collaboration, tolerance, and connections has helped it grow into an entity that can survive adverse conditions that are seen in everyday life.

Our next chapter covers resilience and what is needed in order to increase our ability to respond to setbacks in a healthy manner.

**"You may say I'm a dreamer, but I'm not the only one.
I hope someday you'll join us.
And the world will live as one."**

John Lennon

Chapter 10

Resilience

I received a call from my daughter a while back. Krys had run into ethical issues with a company she was working for and lost her job due to inquiries into questionable practices. Obviously, she was awfully upset and didn't quite know what to do next because she didn't expect to be "let go" at that time. She was angry and truly felt as if she was burned by this model of business.

Instead of wallowing in self-pity and playing the blame game, she decided to be proactive. This incredible young woman spent time in self-reflection, collaborated with peers in the same field of work, trusted herself, and knew she was creative and resilient enough to make it through the trauma she had endured. She decided to take the knowledge she had gained from her last employer and apply it to her own business, which would be based on her core values.

While Krys worked for this company, she had been building a social media presence in the world of environmental sustainability, promoting positive, sustainable change as content, and had been wanting to pursue this activity in a more purposeful way as an influential social media personality. As a result of her being laid off from her job, she now had the time to build a community of like-minded people across the planet who wanted to make the world a better place. Companies with the same ideals were attracted to her, and she was able to extend her creativity to include mental and physical health as it interplays with sustainability.

As a result of her resiliency to this horrid experience, Krys built an active podcast, expanded her social media presence, and launched an online business. Her diligence, hard work, and resilience built a small business that she believes in and is based 100 percent on her values. I'd like to say that she learned her form of resilience from me, but she did this on her own, and I'm very proud of the path that she has taken and whatever path she takes in the future. You can check out her website at www.krystalynngier.com.

Our pothos ivy has grown beyond our wildest dreams. The green vines have grown long and are reaching the floor with light green shiny leaves intermingling with the older, darker green ones. The pot, soil, light, water, fertilizer, room for growth, mediation of temperature, and cleaning of the leaves have led to a beautiful specimen of a plant. Now, the vines are very long and should be trimmed. Once vines reach a certain length, they tend to become a bit leggy with a diminishment of leaves. More maintenance is required through trimming and pruning so that our exquisite ivy continues to be lush and full. This maintenance is a dynamic resilience that students acquire as they learn to live their values as you continue to teach values as part of your curriculum.

What Is Resilience?

Resilience is the ability to adjust, rebound, and recover from adversity. It is reformation in the face of hardship, trauma, tragedy, or major causes of stress. It's the ability to recover from obstacles, setbacks, or difficulties and to keep one's composure in the face of trouble. Resilience is having the strength and stamina to deal with life's challenges as they arise with grace and dignity.

In order to be resilient, we must be willing to address stress, not avoid it. Since stress and adversity can be fluid, our resiliency must follow suit. While resiliency may be a natural reaction to stress for some people, there are those of us who have to work at it. Resiliency can be cultivated, as it is a result of following our sets of beliefs and values, and it can be enhanced through regular practice and mindfulness activities.

Since stress and adversity can be fluid, true resiliency follows suit by being open to the ebb and flow of life and its rollercoaster of experiences. How does someone successfully maneuver through compromising situations that life flings at them? How does someone learn from their negative experiences and use those experiences to grow into a better person? Is this a superhero power only available to the mindful few?

A few traits have been found in those who appear to be more resilient than others. Internally, they tend to be optimistic, flexible in their thinking, adaptable to changing situations, actively solve problems, and have the dedication to persevere with a sense of purpose. Those with these personality traits tend to dedicate time in their lives to learning how to healthily regulate emotions through the regular practice of self-reflection and self-compassion. As a result of the above, they learn from their mistakes and failures and move on to a new level of self-awareness.

Resilience can also be influenced by external sources of support, including solid bonds with friends, family, or neighbors, easy access to resources, social support networks, and a nurturing environment. Having support systems in place to provide direction, moral support, and useful help when things get tough can help one deal with and overcome hardship.

The Story of Resilience

We have covered a great deal of the merits of values in this book. As these values are developed and shared with students, a higher level of resiliency develops for both you as the teacher and the student as the learner. A feeling of well-being can also be enhanced with strong resiliency. Now, I'm going to tell you a story of someone I know quite well—my own story of resilience.

As I write this book, I am in my mid-fifties and have been through many trials and tribulations, just as you, my dear reader, have dealt with during your life, but my story may surprise you. To look at me, you would see a white, older woman fighting the effects of menopause and graying hair. I have the look of a stereotypical all-American suburban woman who has had an easy, whitewashed life and is currently living the life of an empty nester.

Looks can be deceiving, and in my case, this is the truth. Throughout my life, I've felt jealousy toward those who had an "easy" existence, but now I know my journey has given me a deeper level of self-awareness. I feel that I have a deep understanding of those around me and can determine the best route to help others through that understanding.

I'll start my story as a seventeen-year-old high school dropout who just took the General Educational Development (GED) test. Due to previous life dramas that were beyond my control, I had been withdrawn from high school, and upon reregistration a few years later, I would not be graduating with my original peers. High school attendance was required for an additional year, which was disappointing. Since I had been in advanced classes before being withdrawn from school during my sophomore year, I assumed I would have enough credits to catch up with my classmates.

I had been on my own for quite a while, and the high school vibe was exhausting. I had grown weary of the people at a new high school (I was no longer allowed in the Gifted and Talented program) and had chosen to apply to the local community college and take the GED exam. After passing the exam, a friend and I went out to celebrate by barhopping, and I met my first ex-husband. We dated, fell in what I thought was love, and he proposed soon after that. Since he was stationed at a nearby army base, I thought he was steady, trustworthy, and someone I could depend on. We married one month before I turned eighteen by a Justice of the Peace with two witnesses.

Soon after our wedding, I discovered I was pregnant. I also learned that my husband couldn't pass his physical fitness tests. When I was four months pregnant, he was dishonorably discharged from the army, and we moved to live with his family in the Northwestern United States. It was quite a culture shock. He was the oldest of eleven children, all very religious and all still living at home. In addition, his father was abusive to the younger children, and I was not allowed to intervene. It was devastating.

My husband had difficulty finding employment and would not actively look for a job unless I helped him. Out of sheer desperation, we both took jobs at a potato distribution plant where I learned the ins and outs of potato separation. It felt like an eternity until we made enough money to move out of his parent's house. Eventually, the potato gig ended, my legs swelled with fluid, and I fell into preterm labor.

I spent a great deal of time in and out of the hospital, trying to delay the birth of my first child. I was terrified. It was the responsibility of my body to allow this child to survive or not. I was only eighteen, far from my mother, and now my husband had been fired. He blamed me and his concern for my health, and I believed him. Little did I realize that I had married an abusive, angry man, and I had little to no tools to deal with the stress and misery.

Thankfully, due to medical science, my son was born healthy and thrived. I was able to find a job and return to work as a secretary answering phones. My husband became insanely jealous and even more abusive and angry. I finally realized the mistake I made in marrying him, so I made a new choice. I left to go back home with my son.

Within a short period of time, I had a job, and with the assistance of child support, I was able to scrape enough money together to afford an apartment. After six months of separation, I felt that my husband and I had made some amends, and he moved back in with me after moving back down to the Southern States. Imagine my surprise when he showed up thousands of dollars in debt and with an even more abusive temper.

Once he found a job, his abusive behavior slowed, and we appeared to be happy. We had made progress on paying off the debts he had accumulated, and it seemed that all was well. Unbeknownst to me, he decided to quit his job and would spend his days running the roads in our car. I discovered this fact when I asked about his lack of a paycheck at the end of our last month together. His response? He lashed out at the baby, and I called the police for support.

When he left, he chose to abandon his son and leave the debts in my care. I was forced to move into an old, dilapidated apartment, work as a secretary during the day, and clean offices at night. More often than not, I had to choose who would eat dinner—my son or myself. Of course, I chose my son, and if it were not for my grandparents, who helped me as much as they could at the time, I would not have eaten daily. I was too proud to ask for help, and they made sure I would eat a little dinner and send me home with extra vegetables from their garden.

I liked my secretarial job, although it was a long-term temporary position. The people I worked with were kind, and my boss was a very sweet older gentleman who worked as a patent attorney for a large corporation. He commonly had me work on documents in his office with him, and he loved to crack jokes as we worked together. One day, as I was outwardly distressed because of my home life, my boss listened to my story as I cried across from his desk. He stood in front of me, held my hand, and told me that I was much too smart to keep living this way and that I needed to continue my education. I remember vividly as he said, "You are meant for much greater things in this life."

His faith in my abilities and his wish for my well-being were the stimuli that changed the rest of my life.

I began to look into school options. There was a four-year college in my hometown, and although I wasn't accepted as a full-time student, I was allowed to take correspondence courses. These courses were like online classes but through the mail. Within six months, I had achieved twelve hours of credits and had decided to attend a chiropractic college.

In preparation, I moved to another town with a community college system and began my education in earnest, living off student loans and grants. I was dedicated, living in a small one-bedroom apartment with my son, and I celebrated my twenty-first birthday by buying a six-pack of beer and eating beans and rice for dinner.

Building Resilience

How do we build our emotional toolbox? What tools do we place in this invaluable resource for survival in this ever-changing and challenging activity we call life? The adversities of our lives are always challenging, so resiliency is how we go about looking at and advancing through life while dealing with those troubles. Just like any activity, we must practice—much like a child learning to walk. First, babies lift their heads, learn to roll over, and crawl. Then, they stand and begin to walk. Nothing happens without practice.

1. Change How You Look at the World

During the story I shared, some very pivotal moments occurred when I changed my viewpoint to be more positive. I decided to go back to high school after a very traumatizing situation. Then, after attending the new high school, I looked at my options when I realized that high school was not a place I could be anymore. Years later, I began to look toward the future with the help of my own personal angel—my boss at the time. I constantly scanned for life's silver lining. I knew if I were to survive this situation, I would have to continually search for something to be grateful for, and I intentionally focused on the moment in front of me by way of journaling. I kept a diary and wrote down my thoughts each day. In addition, I bit off life's issues a little at a time, making them more manageable in my mind as each day led to the next.

In today's world, we are surrounded by negativity, and our environment seems polar in nearly every aspect. It seems that middle ground on any subject seems to have been wiped away like quicksand under our feet. I focus on changing my mindset every day. I journal and spend time self-reflecting about the positives of my life, what I can be grateful for, and how I can express that gratitude.

2. Confront Fears

My life as a young adult was terrifying. I was lost and felt as if I did not belong, which was beveled into my very being by an abusive relationship. At my final breaking point, I had to make myself face the fear of being left out and alone by demanding that he leave with the help of the police. This had been practiced in my mind thousands of times before I confronted him. Looking at your fears with an open mind can have great benefits, but it must be done slowly and consciously.

Avoidance of fears may make you feel better in the short term, but it can make life situations worse. It is important to think about your fears and recognize the discomfort they make you feel. Gradually expose yourself to the fear. If it is too hard to do on your own, it would be a good idea to get professional help, which is something I have also done.

3. Practice Self-Compassion

During the wee hours of the morning and while in the car stuck in rush hour traffic, I would calm my mind by being kind to myself. For years, I felt that it was my fault and that I deserved to be abused, and later, I thought that I deserved to be hungry. It took many hours of journaling and self-reflection to realize that I didn't deserve to be treated that way. After all, there were always segments on the news about domestic abuse, and I had a hotline I could call if necessary, although I never called it. Being kind to myself was difficult, but I did manage to use this tool to become more resilient.

As discussed in Chapter 5, self-compassion is a technique to approach our pain in a balanced fashion with mindfulness and tenderness toward ourselves. By treating oneself with the same consideration as we would a friend, we can see things differently and gain a greater understanding of our circumstances. This helps us face suffering while accepting the reality of the moment as it is.

4. Adaptability

I became adaptable to change at an early age, prior to this story, so I have always thrived when I had to adapt to changes in my life. It seemed natural. I moved around without help numerous times to both different cities and different homes, and I had other major life changes, such as getting married at an early age and adjusting to living with and without abuse regularly. On top of that, I had a child at an early age and became a single mother without support.

Adaptability is a personality trait related to resilience in that being able to quickly change and overcome obstacles, as well as being open to new options, are basic qualities of being able to adjust to new conditions. While resilience refers to the capacity to return to a prior, more positive state following adversity or struggle, adaptability refers to the ability to change in order to cope under novel circumstances.

5. Forgiveness

This is a tough one. I was not able to work on this aspect in my story, but I have spent a great deal of time on it since that time of my life. It hasn't been easy. Becoming a forgiving person entails making a conscious choice to let go of bitterness and rage. I have integrated this personal value as part of compassion and self-compassion. First, you must recognize what person or act needs forgiveness and make a conscious choice to forgive. During my life, therapists helped me with techniques, but it was up to me to forgive and release the control that the person or situation had over me during my life.

As Alexander Pope stated in the early eighteenth century, "To err is human, to forgive divine." We must recognize that we are human and fallible, and we must treat our mistakes by facing them and moving on without judgment of ourselves and others. Because fallibility is a natural aspect of being human, we must realize that others may treat us poorly, but they are human as well and can make mistakes. Having the ability to forgive is an important aspect of resilience because when you forgive others, you also forgive yourself and don't allow the resentment and hurt to fester over long periods. As you work to learn your self-awareness, your well-being will also be lifted as part of the forgiveness process.

6. **Meditation**

This is a technique I wish I had known when I was a young woman struggling with survival in my late teens and early twenties. We have discussed meditation in Chapter 4 in-depth and the benefits that it holds both physically and mentally. Meditation is a mindfulness technique used by a great number of people throughout the ages and has been shown to help with increased resilience.

Increasing resilience with this technique requires time to quiet your mind, focusing on the emotions of both success and failure, and then taking the time to also observe yourself objectively without bias. As you let the events you are encountering flow through your consciousness, you will develop a new way to positively affect the way you feel about your situation.

7. **Social Connections**

In my story earlier in this chapter, social connections played a huge role in my resilience. I had family and friends that held me up and made sure that I was fed. Although I was estranged from them during periods when I lived in the Northwestern United States with my ex-husband's family, they were available when I returned home. They made me feel better about my tortuous experiences.

We spoke extensively about connections in Chapter 9. The happy boost that comes from engaging with other people is crucial to general health and well-being and plays a vital part in establishing resilience, much like optimism and gratitude. Having a sense of belonging and friendships are important for our physical well-being and are considered basic psychological requirements. Close and personal relationships are important, but studies have shown that even weak ties with others can have positive effects on people and their levels of resilience.

Resilience Exercise:

Answer the following questions reflectively in your journal. These questions apply to you as a person but can also be modified for use in the classroom with students.

Gratitude/Change of Mindset

1. Write five things that you are grateful for in your life. These can be anything that deals with you as a person. Write as much as you wish about your gratitude on this subject. You are not boasting. You are showing thankfulness—a key personality trait/value of a resilient person.

2. Write two to three sentences about something that you are not happy about. Write three ways that you can be grateful for that situation. You are looking for the silver lining, the positive, in a situation that makes you unhappy.

Identifying Strengths

1. Write two to three sentences about an issue you had to overcome.

2. What resiliency strategies did you call upon?

3. What did you learn about yourself?

4. How can you use this strength now?

Forgiveness

Read this fully before performing this exercise.

1. Close your eyes.

2. Visualize the person you need to forgive in your mind directly in front of you.

3. Reprimand this person in your mind for the wrongs they have done to you.

4. Stop reprimanding after one to two minutes.

5. Imagine you are the person you are forgiving, and think of reasons why they treated you this way. Really think of a reason, whether it applies to you personally or not.

6. Think of the lessons that you have learned from this situation and this process of forgiveness.

7. In your mind, shake the person's hand or give them a hug and imagine saying, "I forgive you."

8. Write in your journal how this made you feel.

After answering the questions above, take a short break to reflect on what you have written. If you are working individually, add any additional notes that may have come to mind. If performing this exercise in a group or with students, have another member of the study group share their answers as you listen without judgment, and then you do the same.

Resilience Exercise Conclusion:

How did the questions make you feel? How were you able to find the positive in the negative situation you wrote about? Reflect on the strengths you didn't know you had. Were you able to visualize shaking the person's hand at the end of the forgiveness exercise?

Resiliency is using the best part of ourselves to overcome obstacles and learn from problems and setbacks. It takes many values firmly in place to make us more resilient. Using these techniques to build on core values, anyone can strengthen resiliency. It takes time and effort, but it is worth it.

Chapter 10 Summary

Resilience is the ability to adapt, rebound, and recover from trials and tribulations dealt with in life. Resilient personalities have been found to be able to change their mindset over an issue, focusing on converting negative occurrences to positive ones. They also healthily confront their fears, practice self-compassion, are adaptable, practice forgiveness, mindfully meditate, spend time in self-reflection, and have positive social connections in their lives. By practicing these valuable traits, resiliency to setbacks can be built.

Now that we have covered various personality aspects of a person who is resilient, you can bring it to the classroom and model it as the teacher. As a part of this process, you can help students reframe negative mindsets, encourage responsibility, promote strong social connections, foster a growth mindset, and establish a safe place for students to express themselves.

Our pothos ivy is flourishing as its green vines are thick and flush with new and old growth, varying the shades of a young green to a deeper green throughout its body that is draped along the front of our desk. With a pot of core values—trusting soil, reflective light, compassionate water, respectful nutrients, collaborative room for growth, tolerant temperatures, cleaned connections, and resilient trimming—our pothos ivy is full of healthy leaves and vines that can now be propagated and shared with others.

The next chapter covers many values that are useful in the classroom and in life, such as courage, creativity, generosity, optimism, patience, and responsibility.

"Do not judge me by my success, judge me by how many times I fell down and got back up again."

Nelson Mandela

Chapter 11

Multidimensional Values

For many years, I've talked about how I should write a book, but I always thought it would be about my life experiences as I struggled through one tumultuous issue after another as a child and younger adult. When I finally grasped the courage and let my creativity take hold, I sat down and began to type. It was a challenge, something I had never done before, and required a level of creativity and patience with myself that I have found refreshing some days and frustrating on others. You see, I am chronically left-brained, which means I am excellent at logical activities such as organizing, scrutinizing, and classifying. Taking that knowledge and applying creativity to form an optimistic spin has been a terrifying and exhilarating experience.

Writing has expressed what is in my heart. It has brought out my vulnerabilities and opened me to ridicule and negativity in my world that may not be welcome. I've always been hypersensitive to criticism and have taken too much responsibility for being less than perfect. I'm not a perfectionist, and I'm not a people pleaser. I've just been harsh with myself and less than generous with others when criticized in the past. This is something I have worked on and will continue to work on long after writing this book.

We have discussed several core values that are widely appreciated by society, and I've intermingled related values along the way. This chapter is dedicated to "other values" such as courage, creativity, generosity, optimism, patience, and responsibility—values that I find just as important as the ones discussed earlier in this book.

Our pothos ivy is absolutely gorgeous as it drapes the front of our desk. The students also enjoy its most recent growth which has enveloped the front of the classroom with its long vines and multicolor of green. With a large pot of core values, soil filled with trust, light brimming with reflection, water replete with compassion, nutrients permeating with respect, growing room abundant with collaboration, temperature flush with tolerance, cleaning of leaves bountiful with resilience, we now have a plant that is ready to share magnanimously as propagation. The vines can be cut and trimmed and added to water for roots to grow within. Those roots can continue to grow with the plant in water, but as with all pothos ivies and not living our core values, this will stunt its growth. The sharing of our core values with others in our chosen profession and in our personal lives will continue to personify our pothos ivy.

Courage

Courage is the moral or mental fortitude to take risks, face fears, and withstand hardship or danger. We often think of police, firefighters, and military personnel as courageous, which is very true. However, I feel that a child who is willing to raise their hand to answer a question is displaying courage, just as a student who works outside his or her comfort zone is also courageous. How about that child who stands up in front of their peers for the first time to overcome humanity's number one fear: public speaking?

If we treat all acts by students with a growth mindset, they would know their worth and the level of courage that is being expressed in such acts. Your recognition as a teacher toward a student doesn't have to be a parade or celebratory party. It can simply be a high-five or a big, honest smile. That's all it takes—honesty in observance of the courage to stand up and do something different and new.

At one of the schools where I taught, I was the environmental teacher for many years. With the help of students, I was able to establish an active environmental club that cleaned parks, made plastic yarn out of single-use plastic bags, and inspired recycling on our campus. During the years of COVID-19, we continued to have meetings online and plan for future activities when we would be able to meet again. One of the girls who was passionate about the environment was very shy as an underclassman, but as she grew older, her strength grew, and her courageousness began to shine through. In her sophomore year, she lost the presidency in an election, but as a junior, she tried again and won to become the president during her senior year of high school. Her tenacity, determination, and fortitude were displayed for all to see, and she was an excellent president of this club.

Courage is the willingness to tackle new and different things. To show zest and flavor in the creativity of something wholly new or partly different, it doesn't matter. Courage is the willingness and strength to excel and expand outside our comfort zone, and we, as teachers, are responsible for allowing our students to be courageous and strong as they navigate new material and understandings.

Creativity

"To Be Creative Is To Have Courage" is a banner that I have above the art center in my classroom. Creativity is the ability to embrace a subject, thought, or feeling in a different light. It isn't necessary to create something from scratch or create something new. It is a matter of making or recreating something new for you, and modeling this strength of character will let your students know you are willing to undertake something new to solve problems and that you are creative. I want my students to know it is okay to be creative, to show courage by trying something new, and to embrace whatever they feel as a creative outlet.

Creativity is to take something known—available information—and create something that has meaning to you. It doesn't have to be difficult, outwardly innovative, or different. To be creative is to produce an action or behavior that you want to experience.

When my husband and I were looking for property a few years back, we actively looked for land without a homeowners association. Its restrictions would have limited our creativity, so we couldn't do what we wanted to do without criticism from neighbors. We wanted to establish wild pollinator gardens that brought wildlife to our land and needed the ability to be creative to make it happen.

We eventually found acreage, and during that time of my life, I positively enjoyed the intermingling of natural spirits in my gardens. The colors and growth of the flowers, tall grasses, and vegetables I grew were creatively organized and beautiful to behold on a natural, spiritual level.

Our job as teachers is to encourage students to step outside the box—to even stand on the box and look around at the endless possibilities of life. We are here to help guide our students in choosing which reality they wish to inhabit and having the generosity of spirit to share that reality with others.

Generosity

What is generosity? It is openhandedness, a spirit of kindness, a wish, and the desire to give to others. Generosity is typically defined as the attribute of being charitable and understanding, the readiness to give others things that have significance to them.

At one of the schools where I taught, there was a very large population of students who were on the free and reduced lunch program. Over eighty percent of the population lived in poverty and had great needs that were met by the school's culinary program. I had assumed that these students would be less generous with their time, talents, and tithes, but they were the most generous of all the types of students I have had dealings with. They had been recipients of others spreading their generous spirit, and they knew the benefit of this value on a deeply personal level. These students were openly giving of themselves without expectation of a return on their investment. They seemed to know when others needed help, and they offered their hands out at each opportunity.

Additionally, charity strengthens bonds with others and fosters social connections. It increases a sense of inclusion and belonging. This fosters a sense of well-being as it makes us feel better about ourselves when we are giving. Generosity is a natural way to boost self-esteem as we focus our attention away from ourselves and spend time helping others. At the school I referenced previously, I bore witness to students showing off what they were donating during donation drives and the joy they expressed toward each other as they planned volunteering activities. When I chaperoned volunteer activities, I saw these students become closer to each other as their friendships grew with like-minded peers. Their generosity to others appeared to have helped these students create an optimistic, happier, and healthier mentality toward life.

Optimism

Eckhart Tolle said, "The primary cause of unhappiness is never the situation, but our thoughts and feelings about it." Being optimistic has been a challenge for me until the last few years. I had always considered myself a realist, not looking past the obvious issues at hand. Being optimistic is a value I work on daily by journaling and intentionally changing my mindset to be more growth-based and affirmative. Through daily meditation, self-reflection, and self-compassion, my optimism has grown by leaps and bounds, and I find myself being open to positive possibilities despite available circumstances.

On a professional note, my mindset has always been different than my personal mindset due to my passion for my job as an educator. From the first day of teaching, I've always had an open and positive view of the future of our children—the students in our care. I always lean toward the hope that our students will begin to love learning and work toward learning for themselves.

Optimism is the tendency to see events and behaviors in the most positive light or to predict the best possible conclusion. "Explanatory style" is used to explain how people discuss the events of their lives. Let's say that you have had a bad day. An optimistic person would see the permanence of that day as temporary, whereas a pessimistic person may see it as a bad omen. An optimistic person also sees that positive occurrences originate from an internal source and negative occurrences from an external source. This is a form of personalization of the situation. This thought process doesn't mean an optimistic person is irresponsible; it means they will take the positive and make it personal by pulling away from the negative and looking forward to better times. Basically, optimists tend to see adversity as a teaching opportunity and a temporary phase that will pass with time.

How do you spread optimism and positivity in your life? Your classroom? I do it by smiling each day, welcoming my students with open arms, being patient, and having a positive place for them to spend their time—forty-five minutes per day, five times a week.

Patience

Patience is intentionally slowing mental noise that never seems to slow down—quieting the monkey mind, as discussed earlier in Chapter 4. It is waiting for students to answer questions and make their own connections instead of seeking to fill the silence with data. It is taking the time to use compassionate thoughts to determine appropriate words to speak, which leads to the deeds to be followed up on. It is listening to the "not so quiet inner voice" and allowing it to speak so you can confront whatever it is saying and being self-compassionate with yourself as you move past paralyzing moments of fear into clarity.

Just like optimism, this value has been a struggle for me as well. When I mentioned to my husband that I wanted to write about patience as part of my core values, he openly laughed and wished me luck. You see, when I see a problem, I tend to jump on a solution, and sometimes that solution is created too soon or too fast and causes problems that would not have surfaced if I had been patient. My journey with learning patience involves a lot of journal writing and self-expression through pacing and excessive exercise.

What I have discovered is that there is a boundary between patience and avoidance behavior and that boundary tends to be blurry for me. That blurriness can involve personal, family, work, or community impatience, and I tend to leap into action way before it is needed to not appear to be lackadaisical or indecisive. This is a work in progress, and I have a feeling it will be something I will be working on for the rest of my life.

To be values-inclusive educators in our classrooms and values-driven in our lives, we need to be self-aware of what causes us to be overly patient or impatient and act too quickly. As Thomas Edison stated, "I have not failed. I've just found 10,000 ways that won't work." We must learn the boundaries between patience and impatience to bring about change in the classroom that is values-based.

Responsibility

I tend to follow many of my graduated students on social media, and I have been spending time scrolling through posts. Of course, I tend to get lost down the rabbit hole as many people do, and as I keep scrolling, I lose myself in time as I watch short videos of people I do and don't know. All I can say is that if future generations gauge our level of ethical responsibility on what I have witnessed, they will determine we are irresponsible and self-consumed.

150

To be responsible is to be trustworthy and to take obligations seriously, whatever those obligations might be. It gives people a feeling of confidence, purpose, and accountability, and it demonstrates commitment. Accepting personal accountability entails taking ownership of your choices, actions, and results. It involves realizing that you can influence events and that you are in charge of your own life.

A responsible person does not search for others to blame, and they consider the consequences of not following through with actions. I know that I have heard just about every excuse under the sun, including the elusive "My dog ate my homework." I'm sure you have plenty of examples as well. How do we help students become more responsible for their actions?

Modeling responsibly is the easiest way to demonstrate this value, but we always need more refined techniques that guide our students to the finish line. Stressing punctuality, helping students become organized, and providing positive feedback when showing consistent behaviors are all beneficial, but what else can be done?

Goal-setting in creative ways is my go-to. I have had students create vision boards as part of their classroom notebooks. This allows autonomy and creativity in their designs as they created short-term goals on a notebook they would use each day in class. I've also had them set short-term goals, plan how to reach those goals, and analyze the outcomes of those goals throughout the year.

Other techniques have been discussed in this book, such as collaboration and teamwork. Additional avenues include trust, reflection, compassion, respect, tolerance, and connections as they develop resilience. Everything we have discussed in this book can lead to a higher level of responsibility, which can make an educator's job ever so much easier.

Multidimensional Value Exercises:

Read the instructions, complete the following activities on your own, and then answer the reflective questions in your journal. These questions apply to you as a person but can also be modified for use in the classroom with students.

After answering the questions in each section, take a short break to reflect on what you have written. If you are working individually, add any additional notes that may have come to mind. If performing this exercise in a group, have another member of the study group share their answers as you listen without judgment, and then you do the same.

Body Scanning

1. Start by getting comfortable. Lie down or sit in a position with your legs and arms uncrossed.

2. Close your eyes and concentrate on your breath. Fill your lungs completely and exhale completely a few times. Rectangular breathing may be helpful to get you started.

3. Focus on different parts of your body and relax the area as completely as you can.

   a. Start at the top of your head and mentally travel down to your shoulders.

   b. Continue down each arm to your elbows, then down to your hands. Clench your hands tightly, then relax them completely.

c. Concentrate on your upper back and chest. Then, move to your abdominal area and lower back. Clench your abdominal muscles tightly, then relax them.

d. Move your focus to your thighs—both the front and the back. Straighten your legs and bend your legs, then relax the muscles you just contracted.

e. Move to your knees and lower legs. Flex your foot, then point your toes and concentrate on relaxing those muscles.

f. Think of your feet. Stretch the muscles of your feet by extending your toes and then flexing your toes. Relax your feet.

g. Breathe calmly for a moment.

h. Slowly scan your body, starting with your feet and working up to the crown of your head. Hover over any areas that continue to be tense or tight and focus on relaxing that area of your body.

i. Pay attention to any areas that are sensitive to pain or discomfort. Acknowledge that those areas of your body are uncomfortable and accept this sensation without criticism. Notice your emotions as you move your mind through your body and let the emotions pass.

j. Don't forget to calmly breathe.

4. Slowly open your eyes and bring your attention back to your surroundings.

Body Scanning Reflection Questions:

1. In your journal, write how this made you feel.

   a. Did it relax you or make you feel uneasy?

   b. What part of your body was overly tense? How difficult was it to acknowledge it and move on without stopping?

   c. How can you use this to help you recenter during the school day?

Awareness Sensing:

1. Notice five things that you can see. Choose things that you don't normally notice to observe. Really see these five things and notice the nuances of the subject of your attention.

2. Notice four things that you can feel. Be aware of four things that your body feels, such as the way your seat feels or the way the fan is blowing air currents across your face. Feel these four things deeply and take note of the subtleties in what you are feeling.

3. Notice three things you can hear. Pay close attention to three things you can hear, such as a bird chirping, the sound of the air conditioner, or the breathing of a partner you are sharing this exercise with. Pay close attention to what you are focusing on, and give these three things your full attention.

4. Notice two things you can smell. Bring your awareness to smells that you may not have paid attention to before this exercise. It can be something within the room you are in, such as the waft of perfume, or it could be the smell of flowers if you are sitting outside. Give these two things your

complete attention, paying particular attention to the subtleties of what you are focusing on.

5. Notice one thing you can taste. Focus on one thing you can taste at this very moment. If you have a drink, take the drink and notice the flavor. If you can't taste anything physically, imagine your favorite liquid refreshment. Pay close attention to the subtleties of the taste you are concentrating on.

Awareness Sensing Reflection Questions:

1. In your journal, write how this made you feel.

    a. How did it make you feel more aware of your surroundings, or how did it make you feel less aware?

    b. What did you notice in your environment you were not aware of before the exercise? How did it surprise you?

    c. How can you use this to help your students become aware of their surroundings?

Eye Gazing

This requires a partner. If you don't have one, find a mirror and gaze into your own eyes for one to five minutes.

Eye Gazing Reflection Questions:

    a. In your journal, write how this made you feel.

    b. How did it make you feel more aware of your emotions? What about your partner's emotions?

    c. After completing this exercise, why do you feel you can trust your partner more than you did before?

    d. Do you feel as if you have made a connection with your partner or yourself? How so?

Multidimensional Values Exercises Conclusion

These exercises are ones that I have used throughout my mindfulness journey. You have probably noticed that they are similar to exercises in other parts of this book as they have you work on your awareness. Each can be used together or separately, depending on the time you have available. Remember to be gentle with yourself; becoming self-aware is an ongoing process for you, as the teacher, and for your students, as the learners.

As I was perusing websites during the research phase of this book, I ran across a specific blog as well as a multitude of different mindfulness exercises. Mr. Robert Brumet's blog post really tugged at my heartstrings and really seems to simply explain mindfulness practices. He explains there are three "Rs" to mindfulness practice. The first "R" is to recognize, the second is to refrain, and the third is to relax. He states it is important to be mindful when you "recognize 'thinking' when a thought arises, to recognize 'feeling' when an emotion arises and to recognize 'sensing' when a sensation occurs. Recognition requires awareness. Mindfulness means that I am aware; and that I recognize the object of my awareness" (Brumet, 2016).

Refrain means to "refrain from reacting automatically when strong feelings arise; it means to refrain from acting out habituated behavioral patterns that are based on fear or judgment." Refraining is a process of "not reacting automatically or unconsciously" but being aware of it.

Relax means to "relax the body, to open the heart and to quiet the mind." This is much like many of the mindful values-based exercises throughout this book.

Chapter 11 Summary

Values-based education starts with the teacher's knowingness of their core values and how to interact with these values on a personal level. Then, this can be shared with the students in meaningful ways. By using the values vocabulary openly and honestly and instilling values by modeling and reinforcing the use of values as we have discussed, we can have the classroom of our dreams. A learning environment filled with trust, reflection, compassion, respect, collaboration, tolerance, connections, courage, creativity, generosity, optimism, patience, responsibility, and resiliency.

Our bountiful pothos ivy has amplified its beauty and is now able to give multidimensional values as it can be shared and propagated with others due to its resiliency. The light and deep greens resonate with health and vitality that can withstand stumbling blocks in this game of life. The large pot sustains our core values, and the soil filled with trust intermingles with water of compassion and nutrients of respect. With ample room for growth, it collaborates with its environment with temperatures that induce tolerance, and the clean leaves allow connections with the airflow that are so vital for the creation of glucose for energy and the building of its body.

The next chapter of this book will bring together everything we have discussed, making connections and amplifying the use of this knowledge in the classroom.

"For me, I am driven by two main philosophies: know more today about the world than I knew yesterday and lessen the suffering of others. You'd be surprised how far that gets you."

Neil deGrasse Tyson

Chapter 12

Bringing It All Together

J ust how do we take the material covered in this book and apply it to the classroom? It may seem a daunting task, but if you plan accordingly and monitor your habits when adopting values as part of your educational curriculum, you will create a rhythm as you pack your tote of techniques. The purpose of this information is not to add more curriculum to your plate but to include it as part of the curriculum you already cover so that students learn how values interrelate with what is being covered in class. As concepts are covered, students will be fully immersed in values education.

This chapter will cover ideas that you can use as a springboard to create lessons that include the values you wish to cover in your class. You want your students to be cognizant of the values being covered and why they are being covered. This will lead to students who recognize and adhere to values as members of a community, which could lead to creating a kinder, more peaceful society.

I create my lesson plans based on whole units that are to be taught. I've always done this, and it serves me well to see how much time to spend on the values as I integrate them into my lessons. Many of my colleagues design their lessons week by week, which is also fine—don't change what works for you. Implement the values you wish to explore in your lessons, but remember to insert the verbiage into your lesson plans. This is important because it is easy to let go of the values lessons and only focus on facts and figures and to slip back into the educational dogma we have been trained in, and all this newfound self-awareness will be for naught.

Whether your lesson plans are entire units or weekly, you will need to determine which value to place your focus on and when. This is a new habit that will become an old habit, so don't fret if it's difficult at first.

If you choose the values I've covered in this book, you can spend a few weeks on each one. I highly suggest covering the definition and importance of values as a beginning-of-the-year activity. If the students are in middle or high school, you can use the exercise I covered in Chapter 2. If younger, you can rephrase the values they will most likely associate with based on their vocabulary level or have them represent who they feel they are through coloring.

Student Assignments

Student assignments should stress the value that's being focused upon. After you have decided which value or values to concentrate on, you will need to create lessons, implement those lessons and assess the students. This is no different than the way you have always taught; the difference is that you will have a value focus inserted at appropriate times. Any activities that are collected for grading should be graded on completion, not on the content. This will allow students to feel at ease with their personalized answers.

Here are some generalized ideas that may be helpful as you plan to implement values lessons in your classroom. I've used each of them, and they can be used as invaluable tools to create the classroom environment you have always dreamt of.

- Two to three minutes of mindful activities at the beginning of class, such as meditation, gratitude writing, creating new connections by making new friends, etc.
- Openers where students share with each other how to display the value appropriately.
- Vocabulary that integrates the subject material with the values integrated.
- Exit tickets describing what they learned that day with regard to the value discussed.
- Values-based questions as part of lab reports.
- Surveys to be given at the end of each unit. This can also be an open-ended question on a test.
- Projects/collaboration activities should have a self-reflection and peer collaboration component. Students could honestly rate their own use of values as part of a group activity, as well as rate their peers honestly.

Examples

My background is in high school science and the health sciences, so I veer in that direction when discussing specific lessons using the core values discussed in this book. *On the Subject of Values...and the Value of Subjects,* edited by Bridget Knight, is highly suggested reading regarding examples for specific content areas. I strongly recommend this book, as it is full of wonderful teaching ideas that involve the interconnectedness of subjects and values education.

- **Rules**

Respect. Within the first few days of school, have students help you make the rules that will be followed in the classroom. I've made posters of the most commonly used descriptors when asked, "What do you expect of me as your teacher?" and "What should I expect of you as the student?" You may also find that the expectations stated by students are the same for both teacher and student.

- **Getting to Know You Activities**

Respect, Courage, and Reflection. After completing the Core Values activity in Chapter 2, have the students paint a watercolor visual representation of a value of their choosing. Then, have them stand up and explain what they painted and proudly display it in the classroom or in the hallway outside your door.

Sustainable Cities

Reflection and Compassion. Creating a personal trash inventory over a week's time is very eye-opening. Students spend time reflecting on their consumption practices and assessing if any changes should be made in order to be more compassionate toward the environment.

- **Healthcare Careers:**

Trust and Collaboration. Teamwork in the world of healthcare is a must, and positive collaboration where team members feel as if they belong on the team is good for a patient's health. Have students research a career and create a mind map of how the different healthcare professionals collaborate as a team and how they must trust each other in the process of taking care of a patient.

- **History of Biology**

Compassion and Respect. Create a thank you card for an important person in biological sciences or sciences in general.

- **Cells**

Collaboration and Connections. Use the values terminology to explain how cells communicate and share nutrients.

- **Group Activities Such as Labs**

Collaboration and Tolerance. Have students work in small collaborative groups to solve a problem. In health science, it could be to diagnose a disease; in English, it could be to summarize a written text; in math, it could be solving difficult mathematical equations.

- **Mathematics**

Compassion, Collaboration, and Connections. Students can create a pollinator garden. Design, costs, and maintenance would all be considered. Compassion for our pollinators will help the planet as teamwork is required to rectify some of our environmental issues.

- **Civil Rights**

Tolerance, Collaboration, and Communication. Students can create a poster in small groups describing the various laws that have been put in place to protect the rights of citizens.

- **The Natural Environment**

Resilience. The values that nature encompasses are limitless. Have students research and create an artistic project that describes a natural area that has rebounded after tragedy.

- **Community Service**

Compassion and Collaboration. Students work together to help a group in the community that has a need. This can be a drive to collect goods for an animal shelter or a collection of items needed by the homeless. This could also be making homemade cards or even fidget blankets for a local nursing home.

- **Goal Setting**

Resilience and Reflection. Students write a letter to themselves at the beginning of the school year. The letter should include goals and plans for the upcoming school year. At the end of the year, students can open the letters and reflect on their resilience throughout the school year.

As you can see from the examples, you can use your imagination and submerse values into every facet of your lessons. Be courageous and creative as you make lessons that have meaning for students. Our lessons shouldn't be "sit and get" sessions while the students regurgitate facts and figures back at us on tests and assignments. Our lessons should have a deeper meaning with a true understanding that involves the values at each stage of learning.

This is how education works for everyone. I mean everyone: teachers, students, and even staff.

Imagine that perfect classroom I described in Chapter 2. That is a possibility—it could happen. I have made it happen. Envision if all classes taught values as part of lessons at your school. What kind of an impact would it have on the school culture at your campus? I believe it would surely be a lovely place to spend each day. Administrators could do their jobs—administrate—and not constantly deal with behavior issues. Teachers would be more fulfilled being more self-aware, and students would want to be there to learn as they have also gained self-knowledge.

Our pothos ivy is a resilient organism that I visualize as representing our students. Through the many lessons that involve core values expected in society, we have given our students a gift. We have given a gift of intimate context and lessons that provide a firm foundation of values, trust, reflection, compassion, respect, collaboration, tolerance, and connections. Multidimensional values such as courage, creativity, generosity, optimism, patience, and responsibility have been shared and embellished. Our students are flourishing with hope and joy in their hearts as they grow and develop into the future we all depend upon.

I will conclude this book similarly to Dr. Hawkes in *From My Heart* as it has great meaning to me. "The human spirit is yearning to be released from the shackles of our automatic pilot, with its habitual, ego-centered behavioral responses that can dominate us all, and which so often lead to stress and unhappiness. Carpe diem; we need to seize this moment. I believe that we are at an exciting point in human development, one that invites each one of us to embrace an altruistic, spiritual, and intellectual leap of consciousness that will ensure we all continue to flourish."

We will all flourish if we seize the day and move toward a brighter, more values-based tomorrow.

"We choose hope over fear. We see the future not as something out of our control, but as something we can shape for the better through concerted and collective effort. We reject fatalism or cynicism when it comes to human affairs; we choose to work for the world as it should be, as our children deserve it to be."

Barack Obama

Bibliography and Other Resources

Boccia, M., Piccardi, L., & Guariglia, P. "The Meditative Mind: A Comprehensive Meta-Analysis of MRI Studies." *BioMed Research International*, 2015. https://doi.org/10.1155/2015/419808

Brumet, Robert. "The Three 'R's of Mindfulness." *Robert Brumet: Conscious Living for an Evolving Universe*. 2016. https://www.robertbrumet.com/blog/the-three-rs-of-mindfulness-2

CDC. "Adolescents Are Experiencing Violence, Sadness, and Suicide Risk." 2023. www.cdc.gov/healthyyouth/data/yrbs/feature/dstr-feature.htm.

GSA Network. *GSA Network*, 2019, gsanetwork.org/

Hawkes, Neil. *From My Heart: Transforming Lives through Values*. Bancyfelin, Independent Thinking Press, 2013.

_____ *The Inner Curriculum*. John Catt Educational Ltd, 2018.

Holloman, H. & Yates, P. "Cloudy With a Chance of Sarcasm or Sunny With High Expectations: Using Best Practice Language to Strengthen Positive Behavior Intervention and Support Efforts." *Journal of Positive Behavior Interventions, 15*(2). 2012.

Hougaard, Rasmus. "Four Reasons Why Compassion Is Better for Humanity Than Empathy." *Forbes*, 2020. www.forbes.com/sites/rasmushougaard/2020/07/08/four-reasons-why-compassion-is-better-for-humanity-than-empathy/?sh=285222f1d6f9

Ibanez, Agustin, Matallana, D. & Miller, B. "Can Prosocial Values Improve Brain Health?" *Frontiers in Neurology, 14.* 2023. https://doi.org/10.3389/fneur.2023.1202173

Knight, Bridget, ed. *On the Subject of Values ... And the Value of Subjects: New Thinking to Guide Schools through the Curriculum.* John Catt, 2022.

Langness, David. "The Definition of Truth." BahaiTeachings.org., 2014. https://bahaiteachings.org/definition-of-truth/

Love, T. M. "Oxytocin, Motivation and the Role of Dopamine." *Pharmacology, Biochemistry, and Behavior, 119,* 49–60. 2014. https://doi.org/10.1016/j.pbb.2013.06.011

Mascaro, J. S., Florian, M. P., Ash, M. J., Palmer, P. K., Frazier, T., Condon, P., & Raison, C. "Ways of Knowing Compassion: How Do We Come to Know, Understand, and Measure Compassion When We See It?" *Frontiers in Psychology, 11.* 2020, https://doi.org/10.3389/fpsyg.2020.547241

McKee, Kenny. "5 Things Students Require to Build Trusting Relationships with Their Teachers." *Teach. Learn. Grow.* NWEA, 2022. www.nwea.org/blog/2022/5-things-students-require-to-build-trusting-relationships-with-their-teachers/

Moagi, Miriam M., van Der Wath, A. E., Jiyane, P. M., & Rikhotso, R. S. "Mental Health Challenges of Lesbian, Gay, Bisexual and Transgender People: An Integrated Literature Review." *Health SA Gesondheid*, *26*(1487). 2021. www.ncbi.nlm.nih.gov/pmc/articles/PMC7876969/

Neff, Kristin. *Self-Compassion: The Proven Power of Being Kind to Yourself.* Willliam Morrow Paperbacks, 2011.

_____ "Definition and Three Elements of Self Compassion." Self-Compassion.org. self-compassion.org/the-three-elements-of-self-compassion-2/ n.d. Accessed March 2024.

Palmer, Parker J. *The Courage to Teach: Exploring the Inner Landscape of a Teacher's Life.* Jossey-Bass, 2017.

Pir, Sesil. "Reclaiming Our Space: Why We Need to Move from Tolerance to Acceptance for Inclusion." *Forbes*, 2021. www.forbes.com/sites/sesilpir/2021/06/27/reclaiming-our-space-why-we-need-to-move-from-pride-to-acceptance/?sh=5fb225b83b0d.

Price-Mitchelle, M. "The Language of Respect: Walking our Talk with Teenagers. *Psychology Today*, 2014. The Language of Respect | Psychology Today

Project Implicit. n.d. https://implicit.harvard.edu/implicit/takeatest.html Accessed March 2024.

Robbins, Tony. "What Are Your Personal Values? How to Live by Them." 2021. www.tonyrobbins.com/mind-meaning/our-set-of-rules/.

Schopenhauer, Arthur. *Parerga and Paralipomena: A Collection of Philosophical Essays.* Trans. Thomas Bailey Saunders (1860–1928). Cosimo Inc., 2007.

Sengeh, David, M. *Radical Inclusion: Seven Steps to Help You Create a More Just Workplace, Home, and World.* Flatiron Books: A Moment of Lift Book, 2024.

Sharma, Hari. "Meditation: Process and Effects." *AYU (an International Quarterly Journal of Research in Ayurveda), 36*(3). 2015. www.ncbi.nlm.nih.gov/pmc/articles/PMC4895748/

Starker Glass, Tehia, & Carter Berry, Lucretia. *Teaching for Justice & Belonging: A Journey for Educators & Parents.* Jossey-Bass, 2022.

Values-Based Education (VbE). 2019, www.valuesbasededucation.com/

Williams, David R. "Stress and the Mental Health of Populations of Color: Advancing Our Understanding of Race-Related Stressors." *Journal of Health and Social Behavior, 59*(4), 466–485. 2018. www.ncbi.nlm.nih.gov/pmc/articles/PMC6532404/

About the Author

Dr. Shannon W. McPherson is a highly trained and experienced high school science teacher. She has had twenty-six years of teaching in a wide variety of sciences, including chemistry, advanced placement environmental science, anatomy and physiology, biology, medical microbiology, and pathophysiology. She has also been an adjunct faculty member at a local community college, teaching anatomy and physiology to pre-nursing students. She has taught thousands of students at various levels, which attests to her passion, drive, trustworthiness, and love for her students.

Before teaching, Dr. McPherson was a chiropractor with a growing practice after graduating as salutatorian of her class. While growing her practice, she spent her spare time volunteering at her son's school. During this time, she realized she had missed her calling due to the joy she felt every day as an educator. She pursued and achieved alternative certification to teach science—a field severely lacking teachers. She hasn't looked back since.

A mother of three grown children and a whole pack of granddogs, Dr. McPherson is married and lives outside Houston, Texas. She loves plants, animals, books, writing, and, of course, teaching.

Follow her on her blog as she has faced a transition in her career and continues to share her experiences through the written word, professional development, and as a business owner of "Motivate Your Mind" as a 'Wholistic' Neurogrowth Learning Success Coach.

www.docmcpherson.com

CONTACT THE AUTHOR

Dr. Shannon McPherson is available for consultation, book studies, professional development, and speaking engagements.

For details, please contact her at:

shannonwmcpherson@gmail.com

www.docmcpherson.com